This Time
Together

Also by Carol Burnett

One More Time

This Time Together

Laughter and Reflection

by

Carol Burnett

HARMONY BOOKS · NEW YORK

Grateful acknowledgment is made to Ken Welch for
permission to reprint lyrics from "I Made a Fool of
Myself Over John Foster Dulles," words and music by
Ken Welch, copyright © 1957 by Ben Bloom Music,
copyright renewed 1985 by Ken Welch.

Photograph on page iv copyright © Randee St. Nicholas.

All photographs on pages xi–xiv courtesy of Carol Burnett.

Library of Congress Cataloging-in-Publication Data
Burnett, Carol.
     This time together : laughter and reflection /
Carol Burnett.—1st ed.
        p.   cm.
     1. Burnett, Carol. 2. Entertainers—United States—
Biography. 3. Comedians—United States—Biography.
I. Title.
PN2287.B85A3   2010
792.702'8092—dc22
   [B]   2009041090

ISBN 978-0-307-46118-6

Printed in the United States of America

DESIGN BY BARBARA STURMAN

10 9 8 7 6 5 4 3 2 1

First Edition

For Brian

Our legacy is really the lives we touch, the inspiration we give, altering someone's plan—if even for a moment—and getting them to think, rage, cry, laugh, argue . . . Walk around the block, dazed . . . More than anything, we are remembered for our smiles; the ones we share with our closest and dearest, and the ones we bestow on a total stranger, who needed it RIGHT THEN, and God put you there to deliver.

—Carrie Louise Hamilton
December 2001

Contents

Contents

Contents

This Time Together

Introduction

*

During the past few years, I've zigzagged across the country appearing in various theaters performing *Laughter and Reflection: A Conversation with Carol, Where the Audience Asks the Questions.* It's just the audience and me. The evening lasts ninety minutes, beginning with seven minutes of old Q & A clips from our TV variety show to give the audience an idea of what the evening is going to be like. Then I come out onstage and ask for the lights to be bumped up, so I can see everyone.

Lights up.

ME: Tonight is all about any questions you might have for me . . . about our show, the people I've worked with, moments that stand out in your memory that you're curious about—anything at all. So just raise your hands, and here we go!

It's always a little scary, because I'm working without a

safety net. There are no "plants" in the audience, because if the event feels pre-planned, it takes the fun out of it. The audience can tell it's off the cuff, and through the years people have been pretty enthusiastic—and aren't at all shy about raising their hands. When I call on someone I never know what the question will be. I have to say, it keeps the ol' gray matter ticking and the blood pumping.

However, through the years there have been questions that were asked over and over, which gives me a breather by allowing me to count on being able to tell some set stories. If these questions weren't asked (for instance, if the audience was sitting on its hands), often I could bring up the subject myself and tell the story anyway. (Whew!)

What follows are some of these stories that I've shared over the years in response to various questions. Some have to do with our gang on the variety show, embarrassing moments, famous people, not-so-famous people, family, and so on. Since I'm not planning on doing too many more of these story evenings in the future, I figured I'd write up my favorite stories for my grandkids and anybody else who might enjoy them—who might have some fun and laughs and maybe some nostalgic moments as well.

Many years ago, in 1986, I wrote a memoir called *One More Time*, which was couched as a letter to my three daughters, telling them all about my growing up in a dysfunctional yet loving family. That book didn't take my life beyond age twenty-six. This time I'm emphasizing episodes and anecdotes that have brought me to the present time, although I've also included a few stories from childhood that bear repeating.

Originally I began writing this book as a simple series of anecdotes, but as I got into it I found that I went into more detail than I usually do onstage. I also found myself writing about things that I *haven't* talked about onstage but which resonate with me. Some of them are even serious. These thoughts and feelings just kind of poured out onto the page. They might not be as amusing as some of my other remembrances, but they're memories I'd like to share. So what follows is a kind of memoir peppered with anecdotes here and there. I hope you enjoy it.

Jimmy surprising me on our last show, 1978.

Jimmy Stewart

＊

My grandmother Nanny and I were at the picture show. I hadn't reached two digits yet in age because I distinctly remember my feet couldn't touch the floor of the movie house. Nanny and I were still living in San Antonio, Texas. My mama and daddy had gone ahead to California, where Nanny and I would later wind up.

The feature had just begun, and his face lit up the screen. I couldn't take my eyes off him. He was talking to a beautiful lady in a nightclub somewhere. I'm not sure what the movie was. It didn't matter. He had a kind of crooked smile and spoke with a soft . . . what kind of voice was it? A *drawl*? The camera followed him as he stood up. You could see how very long his legs were. I was sure *his* feet never had trouble reaching the floor. "Skinny as a string bean," Nanny said. After the picture show, we went home to the old house, and I couldn't get the man in the movie out of my mind. He wasn't just an actor like all the others I'd seen in picture shows. This man was different. *He spoke to me.* I tried to explain this to Nanny.

"Nanny, I know that man."

"What do you mean, you know him?"

"I just do. He's my friend; we just haven't met yet."

"That's nice, dear. Drink your Ovaltine and go to bed."

Years later in Hollywood—it was 1958, to be exact—I received a call from film director Mervyn LeRoy. He had seen me in a couple of appearances on television and asked if I would meet with him. I was in my early twenties and just getting started, so naturally I was thrilled by his interest. He suggested that I come out to the Warner Bros. studios the next morning and meet him on the soundstage where he was shooting a movie.

"Why don't you get here a little before lunch, so you can watch us shoot a scene?"

Wow. I had never been on a real movie set. I owned one decent suit, one good pair of stockings, and one pair of re-soled high heels. My purse didn't match, but it was all I had. I took the bus to Burbank. The studio guard had my name on his list and pointed me toward the soundstage. I waited for the red light outside, which meant "keep out," to stop spinning. It stopped, a bell rang, and I walked into a huge cavern—cameras, lights, cables on the floor, ceilings as tall as skyscrapers, and catwalks everywhere you looked. At the far end of the stage I saw a small set. It was up on a rolling platform about two feet off the ground. It was an office—a desk, one chair, a filing cabinet, and a door. The stagehands were securing it under the spotlights.

Mr. LeRoy came over to me and introduced himself. "Glad you could make it, Carol. We just have a small scene to do before we break. Shouldn't take long." He motioned me to a chair out of the way. "Okay, let's go for one!" An actor climbed up onto the set and took his place behind the desk.

Mr. LeRoy called out to another actor behind the set door. "Ready, Jimmy?"

"All set back here, Merv."

6

The voice. I knew it immediately. *Oh my Lord, I'm in the same space as my idol.*

Mr. LeRoy called, "Action!" and Jimmy Stewart walked through the door and presented a badge to the man at the desk. That was it. End of scene.

"Cut! That's a print!"

The movie they were shooting was *The FBI Story*. Lunch was called, and Mr. LeRoy asked me if I'd like to meet Jimmy. He was still up on the set, and Mr. LeRoy gave me a helping hand as I climbed up onto the platform. We were introduced. I was inches away from the face I had loved since I was a very little girl. He smiled and said he was glad to make my acquaintance. He shook my hand. He looked into my eyes. He seemed in no hurry to go to lunch.

What was it about him that drew me to him in such a deeply personal way? I admired other actors—I was a big fan of a lot of them—but there was something about *him* that was different. I felt it every time I saw him in the movies. And now here he was. What I had seen on the screen was amplified a hundred times in person. The warmth. The humility. The humor. The heart. A lump popped up in my throat, signaling the beginning of tears. Overwhelmed, I knew I had to get out of there before I started to cry. I felt like an idiot.

Trying to be funny or flip or whatever it was, I gave a stupid little salute and piped up with what must be one of the dumbest things I could've come up with: "Well, guess it's time to tie on the ol' feedbag!" With that I whirled around and stepped off the two-foot-high set right into a bucket of whitewash. For a nightmarish moment I just stood there frozen, my back to them with one foot in and one foot out. Frozen.

Not wanting Jimmy Stewart or Mervyn LeRoy to realize this was an accident, I decided to head for the door, hoping (praying) they'd think I'd done this for a laugh. I didn't look back.

I proceeded to drag that bucket, my right foot still in it, clear across the soundstage, about five miles. The whitewash was squishing away in my ruined shoe, making gurgling sounds accompanied by the scrape of the bottom of the bucket on the floor. *Squish . . . gurgle . . . scrape. Squish . . . gurgle . . . scrape.*

I didn't hear any laughter.

I opened the door into the glaring sunlight and pulled my sopping foot and ruined shoe out of the bucket. I truly don't remember what happened after that. Obviously, I must've caught the bus and gone home. I don't remember hearing from Mr. LeRoy again.

Wait, though. There's a happy postscript. Years later I had a successful TV show on the air, which my husband, Joe Hamilton, produced. Hollywood is a small town, and my husband and I got to know Jimmy Stewart and his beautiful, terrifically funny wife, Gloria, through mutual friends, and developed a close relationship.

I remember one time when we had a party at our house and invited the Stewarts. Gloria called to accept, with a caveat.

"We're going to be there all right, but I have to warn you, Jimmy doesn't like to stay up late, so don't be upset if we leave shortly after dinner. He likes to be in bed by ten o'clock." No problem. We were just thrilled they were coming.

Our guest list also included Steve Lawrence and Eydie Gormé, Jo Stafford and Paul Weston, and Mel Tormé—all fantastic singers and musicians. After dinner, we all went into the living room, and Paul Weston sat down at the piano. As the musical part of the evening began, I fully expected the Stewarts to say their goodbyes. But Jimmy Stewart didn't get up to go home. Instead, he walked over to the gang gathered around the piano and joined in. It was a sight to behold. There he was, harmonizing with the best of them. Later Gloria came over to me and

Honoring Jimmy at the Kennedy Center, December 1983.

said, "He's having the time of his life. I don't know how I'm going to get him out of here!" They were the last people to leave the party. It was after one in the morning.

Gloria called the next day to say that anytime we had another party like that to please invite them. Jimmy had had a ball.

We saw each other fairly often in those days. Jimmy Stewart even surprised me on the final episode of my variety show, in 1978, by showing up and playing the piano, singing his favorite tune, "Ragtime Cowboy Joe." A few years later, in December 1983, I was thrilled to be in the television segment that saluted him at the Kennedy Center Honors. I sang "You'd Be So Easy to Love," which he had sung to Eleanor Powell in the 1930s movie musical *Born to Dance*. Afterward he sent me the sweetest note.

> *Dear Carol,*
>   *We had a fine Christmas. And the best Christmas present I got was <u>you</u> coming all that way to D.C. to sing to me at the Kennedy Center. Bless your heart. All my love.*
>
> *Jimmy*

That note is framed on my desk at home.

Jimmy Stewart returned the favor a few years later, when I was being honored by the Variety Club. Again he surprised me. He pulled up a stool, held my hand, and sang "You'd Be So Easy to Love" right back to me. As you can imagine, it was a moment I'll cherish forever.

At one point I did tell Jimmy the story of the bucket of whitewash. He was kind enough to say he didn't remember, and maybe he really didn't. No matter—I got a laugh out of him when I told him about it, even if it was years later.

I will always feel like Jimmy Stewart was a part of me. There was some strange connection there that drew a little girl to him all those years ago in that darkened San Antonio movie house, when I first realized that I knew him.

And yes, Nanny, he was my friend.

And dreams really can come true.

But I'm getting ahead of myself . . .

Early Days in Hollywood

*

Nanny—my grandmother—raised me. She was my mama's mama. She is the one I pull my ear for on television (still, to this very day). It began as a way of saying "hello" and "I love you." Later, it also included "Your check is on the way."

I learned years later that Nanny had been quite the coquette in her time, having had six husbands. She was also a Christian Scientist who happened to be a hypochondriac. As a little girl I often prayed for her, and if that didn't work, she would hit the aspirin bottle. When we'd wake up in the morning, I would ask her how she'd slept. Instead of replying, "I didn't close my eyes," she'd feel for her pulse, sigh, and say, "Well, y'know, I just never quite *missed* myself."

Nanny and I moved to California from Texas when I was seven, to be with my mama. The two of us lived in a one-room apartment with a pull-down Murphy bed, while Mama lived down the hall with my baby sister, Chris. Mama and Daddy were divorced, but he would come to see us often. He had a drinking problem, but he was a good-natured drunk. Tall and lanky, he looked a lot like Jimmy Stewart. I often think that that might have been the connection I felt when I first saw Jimmy on the screen: a sober Daddy. Unfortunately, my own father wasn't sober long enough to hold down a steady job, so we wound up on what in those days was known as "relief."

We were poor, but so was everyone else in our neighborhood around Yucca and Wilcox, one block north of Hollywood Boulevard (but a million miles from Hollywood). Nanny and I would "hit the boulevard" as often as we could, to see the movies. (My ticket cost a dime and Nanny's cost a quarter.) In those days, movies were uplifting. The good guys met with happy endings and the bad guys didn't. The actors in the musicals were my favorites: Betty Grable, Gene Kelly, Fred Astaire and Ginger Rogers, Rita Hayworth, Mickey Rooney and Judy Garland. Everything was beautiful in the movies.

After the movie was over, Nanny and I would go into the ladies' room and steal the toilet paper out of the stalls (she'd put the rolls into an empty shopping bag to take home), and we'd be set for another month. Then Nanny and I would hightail it back to our one room. I'd meet my best friend, Ilomay, in the lobby and we would go up to the roof and act out the movies with the famous HOLLYWOOD sign looming on the hillside behind our building. I'd be Betty Grable and Ilomay would be June Haver, singing and dancing all over the roof. I poured all my dreams into happy endings, just like in the movies we saw.

I think that's when the performing bug bit. But never in my wildest fantasies could I have ever imagined that one day I would have my own TV show, where Betty Grable, Mickey Rooney, and Rita Hayworth would be among my guests!

Tweety, Mama, and Chris

*

I was in college when Mama started to have a drink or two every day. Her own dreams of being a journalist and interviewing movie stars had bitten the dust. Early on she had written some freelance articles for *Pic* and *Collier's* magazines about Bob Hope, Rita Hayworth, and George Montgomery. But the pickings were slim, and she never wound up with a steady job.

I was attending UCLA and working a part-time job. I had visions of someday having enough money to go to New York and be in Broadway musicals. I kept them to myself, however.

My baby sister, Chris, was around nine when Mama presented her with a parakeet for her birthday. Chris was thrilled with the gift and promptly named the bird Tweety. Mama had a fit. "TWEETY! ARE YOU NUTS? Every damn parakeet in the world is named Tweety, for godsakes! Don't you want to be *original?*"

Chris was about to cry. Mama said, "STASH! Now that's a great name for the bird. STASH! Perfect."

Chris let out a howl. "He's *my* bird! You gave him to me! He's mine and I want TWEETY!"

They went round and round, until finally Chris won. Mama poured another drink and lifted her glass to the bird. "Okay, okay. Here's to you . . . *Tweety.*"

It wasn't long before Tweety wrapped his little feathers around Mama's heart. He kept her company while Chris was in school, and Mama taught the bird to talk. Tweety would look in the mirror and say, "Pretty bastard," and if someone entered the room, he would say, "Where the hell have *you* been?" Mama even gave him a taste of whiskey, which he grew to like. She would put two shot glasses on the table, one with water and one with whiskey. More often than not he'd go for the whiskey, and Mama would double over with laughter.

Mama would take naps, sleeping on her back, and Tweety would climb up on her stomach, bury his head in his fluffed feathers, and nod off, rising up and down with Mama's breathing. They'd even snore together.

Tweety was still slugging 'em back at age eighteen.

Alfred Hitchcock and the Epaulets

*

When I was a freshman at UCLA I spent the summer of 1951 working as an usherette at the local Warner Bros. theater on Wilcox and Hollywood Boulevard, one block from our one room on Yucca Street. My salary was 65¢ an hour. The girls' uniforms consisted of maroon harem pants made of some kind of satiny material, short-sleeved jackets trimmed with gold braid (mine was too big), and a Shriner-type fez to top it all off (mine was too small). We looked like a tacky combination of Yvonne de Carlo's Arabian Nights character and a Buckingham Palace guard. One more thing: the shoulders of the jackets were adorned with epaulets.

Our manager was Mr. Batton, a tall, thin, gray-haired man with a neatly trimmed little mustache. He was a spiffy dresser—and a wolf. That's what the other girls told me. On a slow night he'd chase the pretty usherettes around the balcony.

He was also certifiable. He never gave us verbal orders. He gave us hand signals he had made up—his own personal Batton brand of sign language. It wasn't that he couldn't talk; he simply

15

felt he shouldn't have to, because this was a more efficient way to run the show. Every morning, promptly at eleven-thirty, he'd line up his troops in front of the candy counter for inspection. There were six of us standing at attention: eyes straight ahead, shoulders back, stomachs in. He'd then do an about-face, march clear across the lobby, turn back to face us, and go into his signal routine.

Mr. Batton would go from right to left, one girl at a time. When he pointed to a girl and held up two fingers, it meant she was being assigned aisle two; three fingers meant aisle three, and so on. If he made the letter *C* with his thumb and index finger, it meant she was to work the candy counter. Every girl was required to salute and march to her post, *cutting square corners.* He'd usually save me for last. He would turn his left palm *up,* facing the ceiling, and then touch the middle of his hand with his right index finger. This meant I was appointed the "spot girl" position. This was the job that required the loudest voice: mine.

I would salute, then march to the middle of the lobby and stand in the glow of an amber-colored spotlight. I was on the alert for further instructions, which came quickly. Mr. Batton would make a gun signal with his thumb and index finger, which meant "shoot." Then I'd wait for the second signal telling me what aisle I should "shoot" the customers to. If he wanted me to shoot them to the balcony, he would turn his palm *down* and put his index finger *up* into the middle of his palm. Bingo. As the matinee customers handed their tickets to the doorman, I would blast out, "Ladies and gentlemen, up the stairway to your right!"

I would stand like this, yelling directions, for what seemed like hours without a break. One time I was dying for a drink of water, and I caught his attention as he was on his way to his office.

"M-Mr. Batton?"

He looked at me.

"Mr. Batton . . . could I please use the water fountain? I'm thirsty."

He came at me like a tank.

"Burnett!" *Lord, he's actually talking.*

"Yessir?"

"Don't you ever do that again!"

"What should I do?"

"You snap your fingers until you get my attention, and when you do, you open your mouth and point to the back of your throat!"

As I said, certifiable.

A few weeks later I got fired, and it was all Alfred Hitchcock's fault. His suspense thriller *Strangers on a Train* was playing at the theater, and I loved it. Every chance I got I sneaked in to watch a scene or two, even when I was on spot duty. I was careful and never got caught. I saw the movie so many times I had the dialogue down pat, plus I had an enormous crush on its star, Robert Walker.

Late one weeknight, when the theater wasn't crowded enough to need spot duty, Batton signaled me to aisle two. I loved aisle duty because I could stand inside the theater and catch my favorite bits of the movie. One of the best ones was the climax, where Walker and Farley Granger are in a fight to the death on a merry-go-round that's spinning completely out of control.

At this very moment a couple came in and wanted to be seated.

These were the days when there were no set schedules for the features. People didn't seem to care if they watched a movie from the beginning or not. Often they would come in and sit down right in the middle of the movie, stay until the end, and wait for it to start all over again, right after the news and cartoon. When the movie got to the part where they had first sat down, they would get up and leave, saying, "Okay, let's go. This is where we came in."

I, however, was a purist. I felt it was very important for a story to be told from the beginning to the end.

Back to the couple who wanted to be seated. They had to be out of their minds. This was *Hitchcock*, for godsakes! There were only ten minutes left! They could go to the bathroom, get some popcorn, visit the water fountain—anything! That way, by the time they got to their seats the movie would be starting all over again from the top. I tried to reason with them.

HER: We wanna sit down now.
ME: If you'll just wait a couple of minutes, it'll be over!
HIM: What for?
ME: Well, it's a very exciting surprise ending. It would spoil the whole picture for you—*you jerks*.
HER: My feet hurt.
HIM: You got a flashlight there? We wanna sit down.

He took my flashlight and opened the door to aisle two. I was close on their heels, whispering for them to please wait. And then I blurted out, "BUT IT'S ALFRED HITCHCOCK!" A bunch of customers, already seated, turned toward us and let out a loud "SHUSH!" Somehow I managed to get all three of us back into the lobby and close the door to aisle two. While I was trying to explain the essence of Hitchcock suspense to these dodos, Batton came bounding down the balcony stairs, straightening his tie and his hair.

"What's going on here?"

There was no explaining. I was wrong and the customer was right.

Batton looked at me, ran his index finger across his neck, indicating I was a goner, and reached out to my shoulders. Yes, he actually *ripped off my epaulets*. I was drummed out of the corps. I saluted and cut my square corners as I crossed the lobby, changed into my civvies, and walked the long block home.

A few years ago, the Hollywood Chamber of Commerce asked me where I wanted my star to be set into the sidewalk on Hollywood Boulevard's "Walk of Fame." Yep, it's right there in front of where the old Warner Bros. theater was, at Hollywood and Wilcox.

One other note: the old theater, renamed the Pacific, closed some time ago, but a few of the interior fixtures are still intact. Some of the kind folks in charge had heard about the Hitchcock episode all those years ago, and in December 2006 they presented me with the original door to aisle two. It's now in my home. I smile every time I open it to go into the family room.

Nanny's visit to New York.

Remembering the
Early Days in New York

*

Somehow I always knew that there would be a way for me to get to New York and pursue my dream of a career in musical comedy. And now here I was, on borrowed money from a wealthy benefactor and his wife, who had seen me perform at UCLA. The man had asked me what my goals were, and I had said that someday I'd like to go to New York and be onstage in a musical directed by the king of Broadway musical directors, George Abbott. (I wasn't aiming *too* high!)

The remarkably generous gentleman offered me enough money to fly to New York and have a little left over until I could find a job. There were four stipulations:

1. I must use this money to go to New York.
2. I would pay the money back in five years (no interest).
3. If I was successful, I would help others out.
4. I must never reveal his name.

He then wrote out a check for $1,000. I had never seen that many zeroes in my life!

Nanny just about fainted when she saw all that money, grabbing her wrist and feeling her pulse. Then she started thinking of all the ways she could spend it. I explained about the requirement that I use this money to go to New York. She didn't want me to go. "It's freezing in New York. Your blood's too thin. You'll be dead in a week."

I promised I would write faithfully every day. Then I kissed Nanny, Mama, Chrissy, and even Tweety goodbye and set off on my adventure with my cardboard suitcase, carrying as many clothes as I could stuff into it, which weren't many. I had never been farther east than Texas.

Before I left I went to see my father to say goodbye. He was on a cot in a charity hospital, suffering from tuberculosis aggravated by years of drinking. We visited for a long time, and I told him all about the man who had lent me the money. As I was getting ready to leave, he looked at me sadly and said, "Carol, I wish I could've given you that money."

I bent over to kiss him. "Daddy, I know that if you could have, you would have. I love you."

He said, "Save me a ticket for your first Broadway show!"

He died shortly after I got to New York. It was the summer of 1954.

Stretching Pennies

*

I was lucky to get a room at the Rehearsal Club, a four-story brownstone in midtown Manhattan that housed twenty-five female show business hopefuls. I was assigned to a room furnished with five cots and five dressers—and shared by five young women. One closet. One bathroom. *Five* women. I was given the corner cot and dresser. The bathroom always had newly washed stockings, panties, and bras hanging on the towel rods. The closet looked like it had exploded, leaving skirts, blouses, coats, sweaters, and shoes piled on top of one another from ceiling to floor. In a funny way, I felt right at home, because that was the way Nanny had always kept house. Room and board? Eighteen dollars a week.

The Rehearsal Club was famous. The movie and play *Stage Door* were based on this legendary building. The place was sponsored by several high-powered professional New York women, which accounted for the low rent. The requirement for living there was that you had to be pursuing a theatrical career. If you weren't fortunate enough to have a full-time job in your chosen profession, you were allowed to work part-time in other areas to meet the rent. However, you had to prove that you were actively making the rounds: going to auditions, studying (voice, acting, dance, etc.), and trying to land an agent.

My college sweetheart, Don Saroyan, had followed me to New York and found a place to live across the street from the club, rooming with two other members of his UCLA cohort. His goal was to be a Broadway director.

The club was also very proper; no men allowed beyond the downstairs parlor.

* * *

I got a part-time job working four days a week as a hatcheck girl in a ladies' tearoom: Susan Palmer's Restaurant, on West Forty-ninth Street. I don't know what I was thinking. After I got the job, it became clear that women don't usually check their hats. Fortunately, the holidays were approaching, and the ladies loved to shop; I earned a quarter every time they checked a package. I averaged $30 a week, which left me with $12 to splurge after paying rent at the club. I was never hungry, though. The restaurant fed me lunch, and the club included three squares in the $18 rent.

Winter was upon us, however, and I needed a warm coat. I had never needed one in California, but I sure had to have one in New York. Nanny managed to send me $20, so I took the subway downtown to S. Klein's department store, famous for its low prices, and managed to claw my way through the hordes of shoppers hunting for bargains. I wound up with a black-and-white number made of some kind of nubby material. I tried it on and it felt heavy and warm. I also thought it was quite attractive, but when I modeled it back at the club one of my roommates, Joyce, opined, "It looks like unborn linoleum." That's all I could think of the rest of the winter, ducking Joyce every time I wore it.

I was thrilled when spring finally sprung.

The Dress

*

I went to open calls (sometimes known as "cattle calls"), which were auditions where all of us hopefuls (without agents) would line up for hours waiting for a chance to be seen and heard by the producers of the latest Broadway musical that was casting. I'd sing maybe two lines before I heard, "Thank you. Next!"

I figured I had to stand out more, which meant a special audition dress. I couldn't afford more than $5, so I talked four other girls at the club into pitching in $5 apiece so we could buy a "community dress." With $25 in hand, we trotted off to Bloomingdale's to find THE dress that would fit us all. No easy task, because we weren't all built the same, by any means.

We knew that to stand out in an audition the dress should be a bright color. It had to have long sleeves to cover skinny, plump, and average arms. It had to have a full skirt to hide any wide behinds. The material had to have a little give to accommodate each of us in the waistline. Luckily, we were all pretty close in that department.

We pored over racks and racks and finally found a loud

orange number that pretty much met all our requirements: high neck, long sleeves, full skirt. Each one of us tried it on and agreed that this was IT. We plunked down our combined $25 and marched out of Bloomingdale's proud as punch that we had accomplished the impossible.

We agreed that the dress would be signed out only if you had an audition, and then you'd be responsible for returning it to the community closet, dry-cleaned and ready for the next girl to sign out. I wore it several times. I never got a job out of it, but I did get several callbacks for "the girl in the orange dress."

I finally gave up on it when another girl in an orange dress showed up at a cattle call and she got the callback.

I switched to yellow after that.

One Rainy Night

*

It was a Saturday night and all four of my roommates were out on dates. The skies had opened up and it was pouring outside—my favorite kind of weather. I've always loved the rain, and I believe it brings me good luck. I was sitting on my cot listening to the radio and reading the newspaper. A song from the musical *Pajama Game* started to play just as I turned to the theater section and saw an ad for this mega-hit. Not that it needed an ad; *Pajama Game* was the most successful show on Broadway in 1954. It starred John Raitt, Janis Paige, Carol Haney, and Eddie Foy Jr. Best of all, it was directed by the great George Abbott.

I looked at the ad again and something clicked: Eddie Foy Jr. He had cut his teeth on vaudeville and was now the featured comedian in this show. A neighbor of ours in Hollywood who worked as an extra in lots of films had appeared in a movie with Eddie, whom he described as a "helluva swell guy for a movie star."

That did it. The rain, the song on the radio, the ad—right

then and there I decided to meet Eddie Foy Jr. that very night and ask him for a favor.

I plowed my way into our bulging communal closet and dug out my pair of galoshes and the plastic raincoat I had bought at the dime store. I tied a scarf around my head, grabbed an umbrella, and headed out into the downpour for the St. James Theater. I almost lost my umbrella when the wind blew it inside out.

I got to the stage door just before the final curtain. It was unlocked, so I slipped inside to find myself backstage in an actual Broadway theater. I could hear the orchestra and the chorus blasting out the finale. The old doorman, looking like every doorman in those old movie musicals (he was usually called Pops), came over to me. I was dripping water all over the floor, looking like the poor man's Eve Harrington from the movie *All About Eve.*

POPS: Yeah, kid, whaddya want?
ME: I'm here to see Eddie.
POPS: You know Eddie?
ME: *(nodding)* From California.
I looked down at the floor; I usually do when I'm telling a fib. And that's when I noticed I had on one black galosh and one brown one.
POPS: Wait here, the show's almost over.

At that point, I heard what sounded like a huge clap of thunder. It was applause! The audience was going wild. Suddenly I saw the stars running into the wings and then back out front again and again, taking their bows. When they finished they headed for their dressing rooms while the audience was still cheering. I was mesmerized. *Is this what it's like?*

POPS: Hey, Eddie, this kid here wants to see ya!
Omigod, here he comes . . .

EDDIE: Yeah, kid, whaddya want?

ME: *(all in one breath)* Well-Mr.-Foy-a-friend-of-mine-from-California-where-I-just-came-from-worked-with-you-in-a-movie-he-had-a-bit-part-as-an-Irish-cop-remember? Anyhow-he-said-you-were-a-real-swell-guy-and-that-maybe-when-I-get-to-New York-I-should-ask-you-for-your-advice-on-how-to-get-into-show-business! I-can't-get-a-job-'cause-I-don't-have-an-agent-and-I-can't-get-an-agent-unless-they-see-me-in-something!

I stopped to take a breath.

There was a pause. *Please, God, don't let him look at my galoshes!*

EDDIE: You sing?

ME: Kind of . . . I'm pretty loud.

EDDIE: Dance?

ME: I can jitterbug.

EDDIE: Well, maybe I could get you an audition here for a chorus replacement.

ME: But I don't read music, and I really can't dance.

EDDIE: *(eyeing his dressing room, wiping his neck with the towel)* Okay, you can't read music and you can't dance. Then . . . what?

ME: Well, I'm not good enough for the chorus, so I guess I'll have to have a featured role.

There was a long pause before he gave me the phone number of his agent, wished me luck, and made a beeline for his dressing room. The fact that he didn't laugh me right out of the theater proves the point that Eddie Foy was, indeed, a helluva swell guy.

The Rehearsal Club
Revue

*

I called Eddie's agent the next day, and lo and behold I got an appointment! I'd never been able to get past an agency's sourpuss receptionist before.

Armed with my red imitation-leather scrapbook containing my UCLA reviews, I was ushered into the agent's office. He quickly flipped through the scrapbook and then said, "So, what are you in and where can I see you perform?"

Oh Lord, here we go again . . .

"Well, you see, I can't get IN anything unless I have an agent, and I can't get an agent unless I'm IN something!"

He looked at me and said, "Then I suggest you put on your own show."

After dinner at the Rehearsal Club that night, I gathered the girls in the parlor for a meeting. "Gang, I actually got beyond a receptionist and into a real agent's office today!"

Somebody said, "Wow."

I continued, "And you know what he said? 'Go put on your own show.'"

Several of the girls got up to leave, but I persisted. "Why not? We can do it. We'll call it *The Rehearsal Club Revue*! And we'll invite all those agents and producers who say 'Let me know when you're IN something' to come and see us, because now we ARE in something!"

So several of us pooled our money for a rehearsal space, wrote our own script, picked out the songs we wanted to sing (one of the girls could play a mean piano), and had a first and second act in no time. I asked Don, my college sweetheart, to direct the show. Now we just needed the money to rent a hall to perform in. Miraculously, the rich ladies who contributed to the club came up with the $200 we needed for two nights at the Carl Fischer concert hall on West Fifty-seventh Street. We sent penny postcards to every producer and agent in town inviting them to our show, the postcard being their ticket.

They came.

After our two evenings, three of us got agents. It was right out of a Mickey and Judy scene in *Babes in Arms*, and I thanked my lucky stars that I had seen all those joyous movies growing up, telling me no pipe dream was impossible.

That was March 1955. Don and I got married in December that year and moved into a one-room apartment over an Italian restaurant. We got a reputation for being the best Italian cooks among our group of friends. Our secret? All we did was throw some spaghetti and sauce on the stove and open our windows. The aroma from the restaurant below did the rest!

John Foster Dulles and the
Blue Angel Nightclub

*

fter the revue at the club I got a summer stock job at Green Mansions, in the Adirondacks. During the audition I met a fantastic special material writer, coach, and pianist, Ken Welch. After my stint in summer stock ($500 for all ten weeks) I returned to the city and called Ken about getting together to write some sort of act I could use for audition pieces. I was back at Susan Palmer's as a hatcheck girl, so I paid Ken $10 a session in quarters and dimes. Don was driving a cab to make ends meet.

That call to Ken Welch was one of the best phone calls I ever made. He and his talented wife, Mitzie, became two of my closest friends, and have continued to write brilliant musical special material for more than fifty years. They've won a number of well-deserved Emmys, several of them for the musical specials they created for me.

In 1957 Ken and I auditioned our musical-comedic material at the Blue Angel nightclub, which was the "in" cabaret, over on the East Side of Manhattan. I was hired! The club featured four different acts a night, each about twenty minutes, and I was one of them. I worked there for several weeks, and the owner said he'd like to keep me on, but we would need some new material. Then Ken came up with a very funny idea for a number. It was during the height of the Elvis craze, and the song he wrote was about a young girl going ape—not over a rock star, but over our then secretary of state, John Foster Dulles.

As far as his public image was concerned, Mr. Dulles was aptly named. He wore glasses, a fedora, and a heavy coat, and he never smiled. In fact, he sported a very dour expression most of the time. Uptight and ultra-conservative—that was our secretary of state. Some people in the media went so far as to call him a "pickle puss."

He was the least likely candidate for anyone to swoon over, which was what made the number so funny. We decided to open our new act with it. I sang the first line, "I made a fool of myself over John Foster Dulles," and the audience started laughing right off the bat. It was an instant hit.

Television came knocking on the door. Jack Paar booked me on his show twice that next week, and I performed the song again on *The Ed Sullivan Show* the following Sunday. Three times in one week! By the time Monday rolled around, the song and I were the talk of the town. Newspapers, front-page stuff. NBC had received hundreds of calls, some protesting that the number was in poor taste and others saying it was a riot. Reviewers raved, and there was even a tongue-in-cheek editorial in the *New York Times* by James Reston: was the song pro-Republican or anti-Republican?

A week later, Mr. Dulles happened to go on *Meet the Press.* The hour was almost over, but there was one final question: "Mr. Secretary, what's going on between you and the young lady who sings that love song about you?" I was glued to the set. He kind of smiled . . . an actual *smile*—I swear I could see a twinkle in his eye. He said, "I make it a policy never to discuss matters of the heart in public." After that, nobody could tell *me* he didn't have a sense of humor.

All of a sudden I was famous: the flavor of the month. People were lined up around the block to get a booth at the Angel, even on a usually slow Monday night, to see *me*. I was lapping it up. My contract had been extended, and I was walking on air. While I was getting ready in my dressing room ("Let's see, should I wear the black or the red tonight?"), I heard the audience filling up the room downstairs. I realized my usual nervousness had disappeared—no butterflies in my stomach anymore before going onstage—and it felt great. Hallelujah! Cool as a cucumber, I finished blotting my lipstick, and then I actually winked at myself in the mirror.

I was introduced and sauntered onstage in my red outfit. The audience greeted me with the huge round of applause I had come to expect. Oozing confidence, I signaled the piano player, and began to sing.

I made a fool of myself over John Foster Dulles.
I made an ass of myself over John Foster Dulles.

Something wasn't right. They weren't laughing. I pushed on.

The first time I saw him 'twas at the UN.
I never had been one to swoon over men,
But I swooned and the drums started pounding and then . . .
I MADE A FOOL OF MYSELF OVER JOHHHNNN
     FOSTER DULLES. . . .

Nothing. Nada. They were just sitting there, staring at me. It wasn't that they were unruly or not interested. It would've been better if they had been, but no, they were paying attention, they just weren't laughing. I felt like I was performing in front of an oil painting. And this was only the opening number. I had twenty minutes to go. My body was heavy with dread.

I decided to push harder to get just a chuckle or two. Not a titter. Then I began racing through the rest of the act, praying that no one I knew was in the audience, praying to die (a wasted prayer, because I already *had*), and praying my armpits would dry up. The flop sweat was trickling down my back, making my dress stick to my skin. Finally, blessedly, the show was over. I made a hasty exit with barely enough applause to get me off the tiny stage and over to the back stairway. No encores tonight, kiddo. I had bombed. Big-time.

In my gut, I knew why. I had been too cocky, too sure of myself. I'd been way too pushy, and it had affected my whole attitude. I simply hadn't been funny.

I headed for my small dressing room at the end of the narrow hallway, where a customer was weaving toward me on his way to the men's room. Drunk. No way to avoid him. We had to pass each other. I knew he had just seen my act. I looked down at the floor and tried to inch past him. *Damn narrow hallway— oughta be a fire law or something.* I hoped he was too loaded to recognize me. I was thoroughly humiliated, and the specter of the upcoming midnight show was already starting to haunt me. I started crying like crazy, and the tears were spotting my red satin dress. (Why hadn't I worn the black?)

He noticed me. "Hey there," he slurred. "Hey, aren't you—"

Oh God. I wiped my eyes with my fingers and looked up at him. He had kind eyes—bleary, but kind.

"Hey there, little lady." He smiled at me nicely. His voice matched his kind eyes.

"Yes, sir?" *Please, God, don't let me blubber.*

"Well, my goodness." He reeled back, bumping up against the wall, and then pulled himself forward again. "Aren't you the little lady I just saw this very minute? Downstairs—just now, on the stage?" He had a sweet smile. I was starting to feel a little bit better.

I smiled back. "Yes, sir, I am."

There was a pause. "Boy, you stink."

And with that he disappeared into the men's room.

The midnight show went better. The butterflies came back and I wasn't the least bit cocky—not that night, and not ever again.

Once upon a Mattress
and George Abbott

*

After the excitement over the John Foster Dulles number died down, I went back to doing some occasional television and continued to audition for Broadway musicals. Not much was happening for me. Ken and I continued to work on audition material. Mama had died, and raising a soon-to-be teenager was too much for Nanny, so I had brought my kid sister, Chris, back to New York to live with Don and me.

Early in 1959, Richard Rodgers was overseeing a revival of the stage musical *Babes in Arms*, which Rodgers and Lorenz Hart had written years before and which had been made into a movie with Judy Garland and Mickey Rooney. I was a kid when I fell in love with Judy and Mickey and the movie, which was about young talents putting on their own show. That film, with a nudge from Eddie Foy Jr.'s agent, inspired the Rehearsal Club Revue.

The producers of *Babes in Arms* were going to open the show in Florida for the tryout period, with the intention of bringing it to Broadway, and I got a call to audition for them! There was a wonderful part in it for a girl who could belt out a song. The

Princess Winnifred the Woebegone, 1959.

character would have two terrific Rodgers and Hart songs to sing, "Way Out West" and "Johnny One-Note." I desperately wanted to win the role.

The day of my audition came, and Ken and I went to the theater together. I walked onstage and stood next to the single stage light, peering out into the darkened theater. Ken sat at the piano in the orchestra pit. I knew Mr. Rodgers was out there somewhere, but I couldn't see him, which was all to the good, because I was pretty nervous. Ken played the intro, and I belted out "Everybody Loves to Take a Bow" from the musical *Hazel Flagg*. When I finished, Mr. Rodgers came down the aisle to tell me that he liked what I'd done. I was on cloud nine!

The director, Stanley Prager, called me the next day and said he would like to give me the part, but I had to come back for another audition. I did, and everybody was smiling. I thought I had it.

The next day I got a call from Stanley, who said he was awfully sorry, but the producers had decided they wanted a "name" for that role, and mine wasn't big enough. I hung up the phone and began to cry.

My sister, Chris, comforted me as best she could. "Remember, Sissy, we've always said, 'One door closes and another one opens.'" Bless her thirteen-year-old heart. I swear, she had barely finished the sentence when the phone rang again. The producers of an off-Broadway musical were calling to ask if I could audition for them that afternoon at the downtown Phoenix Theater, for a little show called *Once upon a Mattress*, a kind of fractured fairy tale based on Hans Christian Andersen's "The Princess and the Pea." The composer was Richard Rodgers's talented young daughter, Mary Rodgers. It was scheduled to run for six weeks starting in May, and, oh yes, the director was going to be *George Abbott*!

My lifelong dream of having my first show directed by Mr. Abbott came true. I was cast as the lead, Princess Winnifred the Woebegone. Mr. Abbott was wonderful to work with, and so was the cast, a group of enthusiastic young unknowns.

The show was a hit, and it ran for a year. Then, over the next several years after that, I performed in it on television in three different productions.

I paid the $1,000 back to my benefactor five years to the day I got the loan, by certified mail.

Babes in Arms closed in Florida. They never brought it to Broadway.

One door closes . . .

Another door closed at around this time as well. After four years of marriage, Don and I parted and he returned to California. No arguments—we were simply leading parallel lives, so we agreed to separate. Not long after that we divorced amicably.

Rumplemayer's and the
Mean Hostess

*

D uring the summer of 1959 *Once upon a Mattress* was enjoying a healthy run, and a few of us in the cast decided to splurge one Saturday night after the show and treat ourselves to a sundae at the most expensive ice cream parlor in New York City: Rumplemayer's, in the St. Moritz Hotel on Central Park South. Even though *Mattress* had been running for a few months and I had done some television, I was far from being recognizable in public. Nonetheless, I was flush with the excitement of being in a hit stage show and raking in $80 a week to boot. I could afford a Rumplemayer's treat.

Rumplemayer's was a pretty posh ice cream parlor. You could spot familiar faces there anytime after the bows had been taken and the lights had dimmed on Broadway for the night. Some folks went to nightclubs or bars, but those who had a sweet tooth and who also wanted to be seen went to Rumplemayer's. I remember having peeked in a few months earlier and spotting Marlene Dietrich in a gorgeous gray pantsuit at the counter, elegantly digging a long-handled spoon into a whipped cream goodie.

On this night four of us pushed our way through the revolving door and stood casing the scene as we waited for the hostess. It was crowded, but there were a couple of empty tables in the back. The hostess, in a blue dress with a white collar and cuffs and sporting a very tight bun in her hair, approached us with menus. She took a closer look, and smoke began to come out of her ears.

"EXCUSE ME! But just what do you think you're doing?" She was looking straight at *me.*

"Pardon me?"

"I SAID, what do you think you're doing?"

Before I could speak, she went off on a major tear. "Young woman, don't you realize that we don't allow ladies in RUMPLEMAYER'S wearing SLACKS? SL-ACKS"—she made it two syllables and pronounced them like a dirty word—"are FOR-BID-DEN!"

She was actually screaming at me. Her pipes could've given Ethel Merman a run for her money. I wondered if maybe her bun was too tight. Suddenly I noticed that the place had become strangely quiet: fewer clinking spoons, less slurping through straws. More than a few customers were watching us, evidently waiting to see if the hostess was going to shoot me. I was feeling like an axe murderer and at the same time awfully humiliated. I was dressed in a nice pair of black slacks, not jeans, but apparently that was still enough of a social gaffe for her to send me up the river and put me in solitary.

My friends and I were frozen in place, but this lady wouldn't quit. I looked for the swastika on her sleeve as she continued her harangue.

"DO YOU UNDERSTAND ME? FOR-BID-DEN!"

I was about to slink out backward when the image of Marlene Dietrich came to me out of nowhere. She had been in SL-ACKS and nobody had yelled at *her.* And all this hostess needed to do with us was to nicely explain the rules. It could have gone thusly:

HOSTESS: *(quietly) I'm awfully sorry, miss, but Rumple-mayer's has a dress code, and ladies are not seated if they're wearing slacks. I do hope you and your friends will come back and see us soon. Here's a mint.*

ME: *(quietly) Oh, of course. I'm sorry, I didn't know. We'll definitely come back another time, and thank you so much for the mint. (We exit with dignity.)*

End of Scene.

Simple. No problem. But noooo.

Astonishingly, she was still at it, not only for our benefit now, but clearly for that of the entire restaurant: "I DON'T KNOW WHERE YOU KIDS GET OFF THINKING YOU CAN BREAK THE RULES WHENEVER YOU WANT!"

You could've heard a pin drop. At this point, the image of Dietrich in pants was looming full screen in my mind's eye. I opened my mouth to speak.

"Please forgive me," I said sweetly (but projecting so that every customer could hear), "but I have a wooden leg, and I'm too embarrassed to wear a skirt."

Dead silence. I felt the entire restaurant getting ready to line the hostess up in front of a firing squad. She felt it, too. She led us to a back table. I dragged my wooden leg all the way across the room without bending my knee and ate my hot fudge sundae while sitting stiff-legged the whole time.

The revenge tasted sweeter than the sundae.

Garry Moore's
Variety Show

*

He's not as well known today as he should be, but in the late 1950s Garry Moore was a television icon. A performer and producer, he hosted his own CBS daytime talk and variety show, and a nighttime game show called *To Tell the Truth*. These shows were big moneymakers for the network, and they were fun to watch to boot. The public loved Garry, with his crew cut and bow tie. When he spoke to you through the camera, he made you feel you were the only one he was interested in. A smart businessman, he was also easygoing and loveable—and a gentleman through and through. The camera never lies.

Garry Moore was also interested in new talent. He held regular auditions at a CBS studio to discover newcomers, which is how I met him. Ken Welch and I auditioned for Garry with our comedy routine, and after that he booked us on his morning show several times. Then his morning show morphed into a weekly nighttime variety series, which was being produced by the same team that produced Dinah Shore's wonderful show in California,

Bob Banner and his associate producer, Joe Hamilton (whom I would later marry). CBS had wooed them away, and here they were in New York launching Garry's new nighttime venture.

I got my big break as a regular performer when Garry called me in to replace an ailing Martha Raye, a wonderful comedienne who was scheduled to be his guest that week. It was a Sunday and the show was to air live on Tuesday, so I had to learn the material in two days. I was scared to death, but with Garry's encouragement and the support of the rest of the crew, I made it through without forgetting anything.

As a result, that fall I was hired to appear on *The Garry Moore Show* every week as a regular, along with Durward Kirby and Marion Lorne. The year was 1959, and I was still appearing in *Once upon a Mattress*. Garry switched from going live on Tuesday to taping on Friday night, which enabled me to do both shows. The moment Garry's show had finished taping (always eight o'clock on the dot) I would hightail it to the subway and dash downtown to the Phoenix Theater, making it just in time for the eight-thirty curtain for *Mattress*. For about eight months I doubled, rehearsing for Garry's show during the day and appearing onstage at night as Princess Winnifred the Woebegone. I was young and had not one but two jobs of a lifetime.

* * *

The Garry Moore Show was my first introduction to television comedy writers. I learned that they are quite a breed. They have a comedic slant on just about everything. I remember one week when Garry's guest star was a very popular singer who was also very fat. Upon meeting her, I recalled all those times Nanny and I had listened to her radio program. She was Nanny's favorite

OVERLEAF: *Durward Kirby, me, Garry, and Marion Lorne on* The Garry Moore Show, *1960.* COURTESY OF CAROL BURNETT

singer. I'm purposely not using her name so I can tell you the following story.

Thursday nights were our orchestra nights, where we heard the band play the numbers for the first time, since we had rehearsed all week with just piano and drums. It was always thrilling to hear the musical arrangements come to life through a large orchestra. On this night our guest came onstage and sang her songs in a voice that, in my opinion, didn't need a microphone. She *definitely* could sing. I remembered Nanny saying, "All great voices come out of fat people." When the orchestra took a break, our guest sat down on a chair next to a small card table onstage, reached into a big shopping bag she was carrying, and pulled out a pink bakery box tied with a string. When she opened it up and took out a large chocolate cake, I thought, *How nice of her to bring a treat for everyone.* She then proceeded to eat the entire thing.

We were all stunned into silence. But that didn't last long. The next day our head writer, Vinnie Bogert, said, "Hey, what'd you expect? She has a sweet tusk."

* * *

Garry Moore was a wonderful mentor, and I won my first Emmy as a result of doing his show. I can never say enough about his kindness, his smarts, and his generosity. Many times when we were rehearsing a sketch, if Garry had a funny line he would turn it down, saying, "Give this to Durward or Carol—they can deliver it better than I can." There was no such thing as a big ego where this man was concerned. Working with him provided me with an amazing education—and I had a helluva good time, too.

Unfortunately, too few people today remember what a fabulous weekly comedy variety show Garry Moore hosted. We did comedy sketches and musical opening numbers and finales, plus we showcased wonderful guest stars (including a very young Barbra Streisand). I suspect *The Garry Moore Show* never made it into syndication because it was shot in black and white. What a shame. Maybe someday some television station will ignore the lack of color and air the show in black and white. I wish there could be a way to make it available on DVD or some other form . . . maybe someday. I think it deserves to be seen again and again. If such a miracle ever occurs and you get the chance, give the show a try, and see if you agree.

My Dog Bruce and The Office

*

I t was winter. Boy, was it winter. A 1960 monster-of-a-blizzard New York winter. I was still doubling in *Mattress* and Garry's show and living in a two-bedroom apartment on the Upper East Side of the city with my sister, Chris, and our Yorkshire terrier, Bruce (who was a she). Now that I was making good money, I could afford to send Chris to a lovely boarding school in New Jersey, and she would come into New York on weekends.

This weekend she wasn't going to make it because of the snowstorm. In fact, I barely made it uptown after the Saturday night curtain of *Mattress* came down. It was eleven o'clock at night and the streets were empty. The snow was blowing horizontally about a hundred miles an hour—at least. It sure felt like it, anyway, and the wind sounded like a pack of howling wolves.

I made it to the subway, took the train, and got out on Lexington Avenue to trudge the three blocks up to my building. The drifts were now taller than I was, and even though cars were parked along the curbs, they were completely invisible under their massive blanket of snow. I finally reached my apartment building and all but fell into the lobby. I kissed my door as I unlocked it, grateful as all get-out that I wouldn't have to go anywhere until Monday morning.

I threw off my wet coat, woolen cap, and sweaters, took off my boots and ski pants, then peeled off my layers of thermal underwear in no time flat. Chilled to the bone, I couldn't wait to jump into a hot shower. I looked around for Bruce, who usually greeted me at the door when I came home, her tail wagging frantically.

And then I saw her. She was lying on the floor with an electric cord wrapped around her little body. A socket had been pulled out from the wall and a lamp was lying next to her head. She was stiff and her eyes were wide open. I put my ear to her chest and heard a faint beat. Her breathing was very shallow. I loved that little dog and wasn't about to let her go. I grabbed the phone and placed an emergency call to my vet. It was eleven-thirty by now, so it took a few minutes to reach him. I told him what was going on.

"Is she breathing? Do you feel a heartbeat?"

"Yes, yes."

"It sounds like she got a shock from the cord, or she may have strangled herself. Do you have any Coca-Cola syrup in the house?"

"Syrup? No! But I have a couple of bottles of Coke in the fridge!"

"Do you have a bottle that's not cold? Not in the fridge?"

"Yes. Yes!"

"Okay, give her some swallows of that. I'll hold on."

I opened up a warm Coke and spooned some of the liquid down Bruce's tiny throat. She moved her tongue slightly and suddenly focused her eyes on me. Signs of life!

I picked up the phone. "She moved a little, but she's still stiff!" I started to cry.

Bless him, my vet said, "Can you meet me at my office in about an hour? I can't promise I'll be on time because of this storm, but I'll do my best."

The man was a god.

"Thank you. We'll be there as soon as we can!"

"Keep her bundled up warm, and be careful in all this snow."

"YOU be careful!" I thanked him again with all my heart and hung up.

I jumped back into my clothes, grabbed Bruce, and was out the door within five minutes.

It was still snowing but not as hard. I had taken a woolen scarf and wrapped it tightly around my chest, shoving Bruce under it so her tiny body was next to my bare skin. Over that I had put on three or four layers of thermal tops and bottoms, along with my ski pants, two heavy woolen sweaters, a thrift-shop fur coat (I wore fur back then), and my fuzzy black angora cap. The vet's office was way over on the west side of town on Tenth Avenue, and I was coming from Lexington and Third, clear over on the East Side.

Miles and miles . . .

Trudging through the snow and slush, I prayed for a cab. At times I would step into a snowbank that came up to my knees. I looked at my watch: twelve-thirty. The streets were deserted. "Stay with me, Bruce. Stay with me."

I reached my vet's office a little after one-thirty. I climbed the stairs and rang the doorbell. No answer. I peeked through the curtained glass pane in the door. No lights. The snow had kicked up again, and I stood on the landing utterly helpless.

Then I looked across the street and saw a neon sign lit up: "The Office." The sign was missing one letter, so it read, "The O-fice." It was a bar, and it was open! I crossed the street and went in.

The scene was right out of a movie, the kind of seedy neighborhood bar you saw in *The Lost Weekend*. Dark inside . . . the bartender wiping a glass with a frayed red-and-white checkered dishcloth . . . smells of beer and booze . . . cracked peanut shells on the floor . . . broken-down jukebox in the corner . . . crooked photographs hanging on the wall above the dusty mirror . . . the obligatory drunk sitting on a stool with his head resting on the counter.

It was the most beautiful place I'd ever seen.

The bartender gave me an odd look as I sat down on the far end of the counter.

"Bad night to be out, miss."

"Sure is. I'm surprised you're open."

"Well, I was going to close up early, but there's no way I'm gettin' out till it lets up some. What'll it be?"

I had never said this before, and I've never said it since: "Whiskey. Make it a double."

The drunk came alive for a second and said, "Me, too!" as his elbow slid off the counter.

The bartender ignored him and poured me the two shots. I just stared at the glass. I had never tasted whiskey before. I took a sip and thought my throat would explode. Then the liquid made its way down into my stomach, warming my insides. I looked across the street. No sign of the vet yet. I loosened my coat, undoing the top two buttons of my thermal shirt. I was holding the shot glass next to my chest when I felt a slight movement and looked down. Bruce had stuck her head out—just her head—and was lapping up the whiskey in my glass with her tiny red tongue, making little slurping noises.

The drunk was staring very hard at us. Through his bloodshot, bleary, booze-filled eyes, he saw a strange furry woman with a black fuzzy head who suddenly had a second, tinier fuzzy head pop out of the middle of her chest and lap up a hefty dose of Jim Beam. He paled and quickly stumbled out the door, mumbling to himself. I saw the light come on in the vet's office across the street, so I paid the bartender and bolted before he had even reached the cash register.

The doctor examined Bruce, and by the time he finished checking her up one side and down the other, her tail had begun to wag. He gave her an injection and told me to take her home and keep her warm.

I thanked him profusely for coming out on such a night. The good doctor said, "Well, I guess it was the Coca-Cola that did it."

I didn't mention the other possibility.

Walking Alone at Night in New York City

*

I remember one Saturday night coming home after performing in *Mattress*. My sister, Chris, our dog, Bruce, and I were still living on the East Side of Manhattan. The sandman had already paid them a visit, but he had flown the coop before he got to me. I was wide awake. At twelve forty-five A.M. I decided to throw on some clothes and walk the three blocks up to Lexington and Fifty-seventh, where there was a late-night newspaper stand. I figured I'd get the Sunday papers and read myself into a stupor.

At that hour, the streets were pretty empty. In those days there were several daily newspapers in New York City, and by the time I had piled them up in my arms, I could barely see over them. I began to walk back to our building. Peering over the bundle of papers I was lugging, I saw a man approaching. We passed each other and I continued down the block. After a couple of moments it dawned on me that he had turned around. I walked a little faster, and I heard his footsteps pick up the pace. I slowed down a little, hoping he'd pass me by, but he followed suit. I realized he was following me!

I still had two blocks to go before I reached the safety of my apartment building. My heart jumped up into my throat as I started to walk faster and faster. So did he. I turned the corner. *He* turned the corner. My building was at the far end of the block, and most of the apartment buildings on our street were dark.

At that point, something shifted in me. I started to get *mad*. How dare this jerk follow me and scare me like this?

It was just at that very moment that he caught up with me and, from behind, took hold of my elbow and said, "Okay, honey, let's go."

I snapped. Turning around to face him (we were nose to nose), I opened my mouth, crossed my eyes, stuck out my tongue, and let out a scream heard up one side of Manhattan and down the other. I followed it up with the loudest Tarzan yell imaginable, and on the heels of that I began to cackle like the Wicked Witch in *The Wizard of Oz*. "HEE-HEE-HEE-HEE-HEE!" I then proceeded to sing at the top of my voice, "DING-DONG, THE WITCH IS DEAD!"

By this time the mugger was racing up the block and around the corner, never to be seen in my neighborhood again.

Nanny and the Auditions

✻

W hile I was in New York working my two dream jobs, Nanny was wallowing in my success. (I hate to put it this way, but those are the only words to describe it.) She was now on a first-name basis with reporters working for the trade magazines, *Variety* and the *Hollywood Reporter*. She called them all the time, acting as if she was my press representative: "Carol's doing this, and Carol's doing that. Aren't you going to print that in your column?" They thought she was a hoot. And they indulged her.

Nanny was also friendly with several extras (actors who worked in the background and sometimes played bit roles in movies), whom she'd corner at every opportunity to give them the latest update on what I was accomplishing—embellishing it to a fare-thee-well, I have no doubt. Quite a few of these extras lived in our old apartment building on the corner of Yucca and Wilcox. I remember as a kid on the way to school watching them leave early in the morning, sometimes dressed in formal attire (evening gowns and tuxedos) and walking down Wilcox to the boulevard, catching the red streetcar, and heading out to the studios for a day's work.

Since I was now working in New York, I had no idea that Nanny was setting herself up in Hollywood as the "grandmother-diva" of all time. She certainly had done a complete U-turn from the day I told her I planned to leave UCLA and try my luck as a musical comedy performer in New York (of all places), when she had said I'd be dead in a week from the cold. I had survived, and now Nanny liked to tell everyone how she'd known all along that success would come my way. Nanny glued herself to the television set every Tuesday night when the show aired, and waited for the ear-pulling signal as we all sang the goodnight song. She loved it.

Then came the heart attack that put Nanny in the hospital. The doctor assured me over the phone that she would be fine— all she needed was just a few days of bed rest and observation. I didn't have to fly to LA. She'd be out of there in no time.

My cousin Janice (known as "Cuz") was on the case and visited Nanny every day. Nanny, in the meantime, had sent out the word to her many acquaintances in the neighborhood that she wanted lots of visitors.

One afternoon Cuz went to the hospital to visit Nanny. As the elevator door opened, she saw a long line of people waiting in the hospital corridor. Some were in costume, and most were reading the Hollywood trades while they cooled their heels. Looking ahead, Cuz could see that they were wending their way to Nanny's hospital door.

Cuz pushed through the crowd. "Excuse me! I'm her grand-daughter!" She eventually managed to reach the door and open it. There sat Nanny, propped up in bed, being entertained by a little girl in a tutu who was tap-dancing and doing some baton twirling, accompanied by her father on a harmonica playing

"Dixie." The child ended with a spectacular split and a great big "TA-DA," arms up in the air, the baton twirling on one finger.

Nanny said, "Thank you. I'll tell Carol about you. Now send in the next one, please."

Cuz looked at her dumbfounded. "Nanny, what in the world is this all about?"

Nanny shrugged and smiled. "I got bored."

Nanny's Visit to New York

*

A few months after Nanny had recovered from her heart attack, I called her in California and asked her if she would be willing to get on an airplane and fly to New York to visit Chris and me. Now that I was working regularly, I was thrilled to be able to pay for her trip. It had been four years since we'd all been together, but I wasn't sure how Nanny would respond to my offer. She had often expressed disbelief about airplanes: "I don't see how anything that heavy can stay up in the air like that . . . it's bound to fall down."

She wound up jumping at the invitation. It would be her first time east of Texas, and she would be reunited with her grandbabies.

I met Nanny as she got off the plane. She was all smiles and waves. The flight had been a good one (it hadn't fallen down), and at seventy-seven, she was none the worse for wear. I suspected she had enjoyed a couple of swigs of sherry (her drink of choice) during the trip. As we were waiting for her luggage, a stewardess who had been on her flight and was leaving the ter-

Nanny, me, and sister Chris.
COURTESY OF CAROL BURNETT

minal spotted Nanny and stopped to give her a goodbye hug. Evidently, they had become buddies during the flight. Nanny lost no time in introducing me to her, explaining how she had raised me and now here I was, starring in Garry Moore's weekly television show! "See? I told you she was my granddaughter! Carol, go on and give her your autograph!"

After an embarrassing pause the stewardess awkwardly asked for my autograph, and I gave it to her (rather apologetically) as Nanny puffed up like a pigeon.

Once we were settled into a taxi on our way to my apartment, Nanny reached into her purse, brought out her little bottle of sherry (I knew it!), and took a swig. After that, she proceeded to belch the rest of the way into town. She could've won a belching contest against the best of them. I hardly took notice, since I had heard her let loose like that ever since I was a little bitty thing. The taxi driver, however, turned around a couple of times to take a gander at this little old lady with so much gas. After Nanny had let go with a particularly loud one, he rolled down his window for air and then swiveled his neck around, with his eyes just about popping out of his head. Nanny leaned toward him, patted her stomach, and explained, "Well, mister, look at it this way—there's more room out there than there is in here!"

He didn't look back after that.

Chris was thrilled to see Nanny, and Nanny was amazed by how much Chris had grown. She was tall, filled out, and a beautiful teenager. We settled Nanny down in Chris's room, and that night we all had a celebratory cup of Ovaltine before we turned in.

It was a happy reunion.

Since I was no longer doubling in *Once upon a Mattress* I had some free time to show Nanny around the Big Apple between rehearsals for Garry's show. She loved Sardi's restaurant because there were always a lot of celebrities there to gawk at. And if I knew them, I had to introduce them to my grandmother or I never would've heard the end of it.

Nanny was in the audience for Garry's show the following Friday, absolutely beaming. She looked pretty good, although I would've loved seeing her wear a pale pink lipstick instead of the fire engine red she always preferred. Also, the skirt to the purple suit she was wearing was a bit too short. All of her skirts were too short, in my estimation, but Nanny had great legs and never hesitated to show them off whenever she could. ("The legs are the last things to go!" she always said.) What the heck—if that made her happy and feel younger, who was I to try to change Nanny at this time in her life? I told myself to get over it. I was turning into an old fogey.

Garry came out to do the warm-up for the audience.

"Welcome to our show, ladies and gentlemen! We've got a great one for you tonight, but before we get under way, there's someone I want you to meet who's in our audience."

Backstage, I was peeking through the curtain, and it dawned on me that he was going to INTRODUCE NANNY!

Bless Garry, there was no one nicer. He walked to the edge of the stage and continued, "There's a special little lady here tonight visiting New York for the first time. She raised our own Carol Burnett! Carol's grandmother . . . where are you, dear?"

Nanny bounced up out of her seat like a pogo stick and yelled, "Over here, Garry!"

The audience politely applauded. Then Nanny threw both arms up into the air, clasped her hands together, and waved them back and forth like a heavyweight champion. The audience howled.

All I could do was shake my head and smile.

* * *

It was almost time for Nanny to return to Hollywood. She, Chris, and I were sitting around the small dining room table having our nightly Ovaltine when Nanny blurted out: "Carol, where do you want to be buried?"

"What?"

"I said, where do you want to be buried? You know, when you die."

"Nanny, why are you asking me that now? I'm twenty-seven years old!"

"Just curious." Then she turned to Chris. "How 'bout you? Where do you want to be buried?"

Chris said, "Gosh, Nanny . . . I don't know. . . ." She looked at me helplessly.

I took a swig of my Ovaltine and said, "Well. Okay. I guess I'd like to be buried here somewhere in New York because I feel I've been given a chance at success here. I'm doing what I love, and I love this city, so I guess here's where I'd be." I handed it back to Chris. "Now, what about *you*, honey?"

Chris agreed with me and said she'd be happy being buried in New York, too.

There was a pause. Then Nanny reared back and said, "Well, if the two of you think I'm going to fly six thousand miles round-trip every year to put flowers on your graves, you're nuts!"

* * *

Nanny died four years later, at eighty-one. At the time she had a forty-one-year-old boyfriend who was a jazz musician in Redondo Beach, California. I remembered the time when I had made a trip to California to move her to a larger apartment. I had brought Nanny some recent pictures to show her. We were sitting on the couch, and it was fairly dark, so the photos were hard to make out. She turned on a light near the couch—a green Japanese paper lantern, which gave the living room an eerie, otherworldly atmosphere. I said, "Nanny, it's not bright enough. Let's remove the paper lantern from around the bulb so you can see better."

She replied. "No. Leave it just the way it is. That's my love light."

Aunt Iney

*

Nanny had a younger sister, Ina. We all called her "Iney." She had a totally different personality from Nanny. She was stoic, robust, and always cheerful, especially with us kids. She would come and visit fairly often. When Nanny complained about one of her mysterious illnesses, Iney would respond by saying, "Mae, nothing's wrong with you; you're gonna be fine and outlive us all!" Then she'd turn to me and ask me what I was up to in school. Nanny would huff and puff and haul herself out of bed to join Iney for a glass of sherry.

During World War II, construction workers started digging the foundation for a new motel, the Hollywood Hawaiian, right up the hill from our building. We were watching a lot of war movies at the time, so every day after the workers had quit, all of us neighborhood kids would go to the construction site and get down in the trench, digging foxholes and pretending we were fighting the Germans and the Japanese.

One time Iney climbed up the hill and joined us! She was wearing slacks and she actually *jumped* into the trench and pretended to be John Wayne at Iwo Jima. "POW-POW! BANG-BANG!" We were all about nine or ten years old, so all adults were old to us, but here was this sixty-year-old woman crouching, ducking, and running around in the trenches shooting Nazis and Japanese soldiers. Nanny told her she was cracked. We thought she was incredibly cool.

Years later, after I had been to New York and was back in California doing my own variety show, Iney came to one of our tapings. My assistant, Sharkey (who later married Tim Conway), brought Iney backstage to say hello. She had aged, but it hadn't affected the sweetness of her personality. I hugged her and asked her to stay in touch.

She didn't.

A few years later, during our show's hiatus, I was appearing onstage in *Plaza Suite* with the wonderful actor George Kennedy for a short run in Hollywood. One night Sharkey, who was still working with me, came into the dressing room saying she had spotted Iney outside on the sidewalk, standing in line at the box office. It turned out she had taken the two-hour bus ride from her home in San Dimas, California, all the way up to Hollywood.

I hadn't seen Iney in years. She had become a recluse. Sharkey ran outside and convinced Iney to sit in a special seat in the third row, saying she'd bring her backstage after the show. Iney protested, saying she didn't want to "disturb Carol." Evidently she had planned to leave after the curtain and grab the bus home without ever telling me she had been in the audience!

There were a lot of friends in the audience that night, but mainly I wanted to see Iney. After the curtain fell, folks began to come backstage for the obligatory congratulations. The dressing room filled up, and over the tops of all those heads, I spotted Sharkey ushering in this tiny old lady, who looked like she wished she could be elsewhere. It was Iney, bless her heart. She seemed overwhelmed and oblivious to the fact that she was the one I wanted to see most of all.

The dressing room was packed. I pulled up a chair.

"Iney, here, dear . . . sit down."

She looked at me and smiled. "Oh no, I don't want to bother the chair."

I don't want to bother the chair!

I forced her to sit, but she seemed uncomfortable in the crowded dressing room. We visited for a short while, and I realized that despite my best efforts Iney still felt like she was intruding. Sharkey called a car service to drive a protesting Iney back to San Dimas. I walked her to the car, and all the time she was insisting she should take the bus. We got her into the car and I kissed her goodbye.

That was the last time I ever saw Iney. She died not long after. She was a special lady, and the memory of her playing with us kids in our foxholes always makes me smile.

Viewer Discretion Advised

❋

In the mid-sixties I would often appear on my favorite game show, *Password*, hosted by the wonderfully affable Allen Ludden, who handed out the game's words and kept our water glasses filled while we played. At first, the show was aired live with an audience at two o'clock in the afternoon five days a week. Later on, it was taped. You'll understand why in a minute.

Password was a brilliantly simple game. Two teams were pitted against each other, each featuring a celebrity and a civilian. Each team sat at a desk with the partners facing each other. Allen stood between the desks handing out the password, which was printed on a card concealed in a small wallet-like purse. We tossed a coin to see who went first. If it was my turn to give the clues, Allen would hand one purse to me and the other to my opponent, both containing the same word, which was unknown to our partners. The idea was to convey the word to your partner by using a one-word clue, hoping to beat out the other team. This particular week, Elizabeth Montgomery was the other guest.

Here's an example of how the game worked. Say our side was

Me, Allen, and Elizabeth on that fateful Password *day.*

COURTESY OF CAROL BURNETT

going first, and I was handed the word "apple." The word would be shown on the bottom of the screen so the folks at home and those in the studio audience would know what the word was. My partner, who couldn't see the screen, was supposed to guess the word after I gave him my one-word clue, for instance, "fruit." If he came up with a word like "orange," which was incorrect, the play would then go over to Elizabeth, who could now provide her partner with a second clue. Elizabeth might then say, "Eve," and after adding up the two clues ("fruit" and "Eve"), her partner most likely could come up with the correct answer, "apple," thereby winning that particular round. After a round was over, Allen would give the next password to our partners and we'd begin a new round, this time with Elizabeth and me doing the guessing.

I will never forget what happened one afternoon. The man

who was my partner was to give me the first clue. Let's call him Louis.

Louis opened his purse and looked at the word, which was also being shown on the screen (but not to me, since I was the guesser).

Louis thought for a second, then leaned toward me and said, "Twat." (For those of you who might not be familiar with the word, it's a slangy and not very nice word for a woman's private parts. I'm trying to be delicate here.)

I wasn't sure I heard what I heard, so I make the mistake of saying, "Excuse me?"

He leaned even closer. "TWAT!"

At that point the audience, which had begun to titter at first, was roaring with laughter. I looked over at Elizabeth and didn't see her. She had fallen off her chair.

Allen, bless his heart, kept saying, "Don't mind me, I'm just here passing water!" The audience roared even more.

I sat there stupefied, trying my utmost to maintain a blank face. After an eternity the buzzer sounded. I had run out of time, and it was now Elizabeth's turn to soldier on. Fortunately, because she was choking so much with laughter and couldn't come up with another clue (or air, for that matter), the much-anticipated buzzer was finally heard, and the round was blessedly over. So was the show, at least for that day.

Okay, now you ask . . . what was the password that Louis was trying to convey?

"Tweet."

"Tweet?"

Poor Louis—he thought "twat" was the past tense of "tweet." Even if he'd been right, we would have lost, since *Password* rules didn't allow any form of the word as a clue.

Did I mention that after this the show went from a live format to being taped?

Fans

*

Recently, I was in the market and a woman came up to me and said: "Excuse me, but aren't you Carol Burnett?" I smiled and said, "Yes, I am."

"I knew it! I just *knew* it was you! Do you know how I could tell?"

"No . . ."

"By your face."

Lunchtime at the
Turkey Farm

*

I've mentioned that my kid sister, Chris, was attending an Episcopal school in Mendham, New Jersey, while I was working on Garry Moore's show. She would usually come into the city on weekends, and on the Sundays when she didn't, I would rent a car and drive out to Mendham so that we could have lunch together.

There was a charming little restaurant there called the Turkey Farm, where people often went after church. The food was down-home delicious: biscuits, gravy, mashed potatoes, turkey, fried chicken, homemade pies and cakes. The atmosphere matched the food, homey and happy.

The first few Sundays we went, I noticed some of the customers staring at me. I'd look at them and smile, and they'd look away as if they were embarrassed or something. I figured they recognized me from Garry's show and didn't want to make a scene. The awkwardness eased up after the next few Sundays. People would smile at us and we'd smile back. Sometimes they'd wave goodbye as we were leaving. They were polite as could be, but still shy. At least most of them were.

One Sunday as Chris and I were leaving, I told her I needed to make a pit stop before we got in the car. I headed for the ladies' room. It was empty. I went into a stall. As I was sitting there, I heard the outside door open, followed by tiny little footsteps clicking along the tile floor. They stopped right outside my stall. I looked down and saw two little feet wearing black patent leather Mary Janes and pink socks with little frills around the cuffs.

I didn't move. The little feet didn't move. Dead silence. Minutes went by.

Finally a tiny upside-down face appeared under my door. She was about five years old with a Buster Brown haircut. She stared up at me sitting there, and grinned from ear to ear. One front tooth was missing. "Thay," she lisped, "are you Carol Burnett?"

Tarzan and Bergdorf Goodman

*

The ear tug for Nanny had become a sort of trademark of mine whenever I was on television, my way of saying hello to her. The other trademark, if you want to call it that, is the fact that I can do the Tarzan yell. I taught myself to do it when I was around eight or nine, playing movies with my cousin Janice (Cuz). We acted out a lot of the picture shows we saw. Because she was the pretty one, I'd be Nelson to her Jeanette, Nick to her Nora, and Tarzan to her Jane.

When I was doing the opening questions and answers for *The Carol Burnett Show* every week, I could always count on somebody asking me to do the yell. Actually, it's really nothing more than a very drawn-out (and loud) yodel. It also happens to be a pretty good vocal exercise. I remember getting Beverly Sills to do it once when we were working together. Naturally, she got it down pat.

Not too long ago, I was in the market shopping for groceries when a little boy came up to me and asked me to do the Tarzan yell. I felt terrible disappointing him.

"What's your name, honey?"

"Brandon."

I said, "Brandon, I really can't do it here. I wish I could, but it really wouldn't be a very good idea." For a second there, before he turned away, I thought he was going to spit on my shoe. But I had a very good reason for this decision.

It went like this. . . .

Several years before, Joe Hamilton and I had fallen in love and married. He still continued to produce television shows plus any special I might be doing. We had settled down in New York.

One day, before rehearsals for our latest TV special *(Calamity Jane)* were to begin, I decided I had time to make a quick run to Bergdorf Goodman to buy a pair of stockings. Bergdorf's was, and still is, a very posh department store. It was right across the street from the hotel where we were staying, and I was in a hurry so I wouldn't be late for rehearsal. The store had just opened its doors, and it was practically empty. I ran up to the lingerie department, found the brand I wanted, and looked around for a salesperson.

A lovely lady appeared: beautiful pale hair in a bun, slim black dress, pearl earrings, pearl necklace.

"May I help you?"

"Thank you. I'd like to buy these stockings."

Smiling, she looked at me and said, "Aren't you Carol Burnett?" I nodded, and she introduced herself: "I'm Miss Melton, and I'm a huge fan."

I thanked her and signed autographs for each of her five grandchildren.

When it came time to pay for the stockings, I realized I had left my credit card in the hotel. But I HAD MY CHECKBOOK! I could write a check!

She said, "I'm sorry, but I'll need some identification."

"But I just signed FIVE autographs! You *know* who I am."

She understood, but she had her rules.

I was at a total loss and running out of time. "Can't you *do* something?"

"I'll have to ask Miss Darnell. She is the head of this department."

She smiled and pointed to a lovely woman way, *waaay* across the floor, sitting at a beautiful antique desk. I couldn't help but notice that the two women could've been clones: hair, pearls, dress, the whole nine yards.

Miss Melton approached the antique desk to speak to her supervisor. After a moment, Miss Darnell looked up, smiled, and waved. I smiled and waved back. *Are they gonna give me my panty hose or not?*

Miss Melton came back and said, "Miss Darnell says that she will okay your check if you'll do the Tarzan yell."

Excuse me? The Tarzan yell? In Bergdorf Goodman? I thought about the panty hose and the people waiting for me at rehearsal. *All-righty . . .* I let go with one of the best (and loudest) Tarzan yells that I have ever done, almost as good as the one that persuaded the Manhattan mugger on my street to give up his life of crime. It was a doozy of a yell.

At that point, a Bergdorf security guard burst through a door, and Miss Melton, Miss Darnell, and I found ourselves staring straight into the business end of a very large gun.

So Brandon dear, forgive me, but now at least you'll understand.

John Steinbeck and the Twenty-fourth Floor

*

I n 1964, my husband, Joe Hamilton, and I, along with our baby, Carrie, and my sister, Chris, had moved to a high-rise on Lexington and Seventy-second Street in New York. Our apartment was on the twenty-second floor. We had heard that the brilliant writer John Steinbeck also lived in the building, but after being there for more than a year we'd never even caught a glimpse of him. Both Joe and I were huge fans of his, having devoured just about everything the Nobel Prize–winning novelist had ever written.

One night we were coming home from having dinner out, and as we entered the lobby we could see that a very large man was holding the elevator door open for us. We thanked him as we got in. In a deep voice he asked, "What floor?" I looked up at him, and both Joe and I said at the same time, "Twenty-two." He pressed the button for our floor and then hit the one for the twenty-fourth floor. The elevator doors closed and we were on our way.

Then it dawned on me: *I'm standing next to John Steinbeck!*

Elevator etiquette has always seemed weird to me. Nobody speaks or looks at anyone else in an elevator. People go up and down cooped up together in a box and do nothing but stare at the floor numbers overhead. That night it looked like the three of us would be doing just that when—at about the fourteenth floor—this tall gentleman looked at me and said, "Excuse me . . . Miss Burnett?"

I was floored. "Yes?"

He offered me his hand—his large hand. "I'm John Steinbeck."

"Oh, I know. I *know*! What a pleasure to meet you!" We shook hands.

He said, "My wife and I have always admired your work. We watched you all the time on *The Garry Moore Show*. Very funny. Very funny."

"Thank you SO much! Ohhh, and I love everything you've ever written!"

He smiled at me. "Well, thank YOU so much." I also thought he was awfully handsome.

I looked at the numbers and realized we had just about reached our floor. As the door opened and we stepped out onto our floor, I *also* realized I had neglected to introduce him to Joe, who was, by this time, looking a bit ticked off.

As the door was closing to go up to twenty-four, Joe nudged me in the ribs, and I blurted out as the elevator door was about to close: "Oh, and this is my husband, George Hamilton." Where *that* came from and why, I'll never know. Joe looked at me like I was nuts, and by the time I screamed, "NOOO! NOOO! Not George! I mean *Joe* . . . JOE Hamilton!" the ship had sailed, and Mr. Steinbeck was gone.

Joe defrosted enough to speak to me sometime late the next day.

CBS vs. My Variety Show

*

So there we were, airing on Tuesday nights for CBS. Even though *The Garry Moore Show* had switched to tape like everyone else, we performed in front of an audience as if it were a live show—no stops and no retakes. We barreled ahead like we were doing a Broadway revue, which was exactly the point. We wanted the spontaneity and excitement that go with the feeling of live theater.

The writing and the musical numbers we performed every single week were certainly worthy of being on the Great White Way. In fact, our junior writer was Neil Simon, whom we called "Doc." He wrote his first play, *Come Blow Your Horn*, while he was working on Garry's show, typing away after hours. Garry was one of his first investors.

After I'd been on Garry's show for a few seasons, CBS asked me to sign a contract with them. Mike Dann and Oscar Katz were the key programming executives in on the negotiations. The deal they offered was for ten years (1962–72), paying me a decent sum to do a one-hour TV special each year, along with two guest appearances on any of their regular series. However, if during the first five years of the contract I wanted to do an hour variety show of my own, *they would guarantee me 30 one-hour shows*. This was called "pay or play," which meant that they'd have to pay us for thirty shows even if they didn't put them on the air. "Just push the button!" was the phrase they used. It was a great feature of the deal, but I really didn't pay much attention to it because I never dreamed I could, or would even *want* to, host my own show.

I was much more interested in Broadway.

* * *

Fast-forward to 1966. Joe and I were enjoying our first beautiful daughter, Carrie, and we had another baby on the way. My Broadway career hadn't panned out, so we had left New York and were sitting on orange crates and packing boxes in the living room of a Beverly Hills home on which we had scraped together the down payment. In big demand just four years earlier, now I was as cold as yesterday's mashed potatoes.

While we weren't in the poorhouse, it was obvious we had to do something. It was the week between Christmas and New Year's. Nineteen sixty-seven was a few days away, which meant that nearly five years had flown by since we'd made the contract with CBS. Time was running out on our pay-or-play clause. Joe and I looked around the living room, looked at each other, and decided to make the call.

In New York, Mike Dann picked up the phone.

"Hey, Carol! How are you guys? Have a good Christmas?"

"Yes, thanks, Mike. Hey, I'm calling about pushing that button."

Friendly but obviously in the dark, he said, "Huh?"

"The button, Mike, you know . . . where I get to do thirty one-hour comedy-variety shows? In the first five years of my contract? Remember that part of our deal?"

Mike wasn't being coy. He honestly didn't remember that clause. I handed the phone to Joe, who explained it in great detail. Mike said he'd get right back to us. I'm guessing that more than a few lawyers were called away from holiday parties that night.

The next morning Mike called back and said, "Well, yes, I can see why you called. But really, I don't think the hour thing is the best way to go. Comedy-variety shows are traditionally hosted by men. Gleason, Caesar, Benny, Berle, and now Dean . . . it's really not for a gal. Dinah's show was mostly music."

I responded, "But comedy-variety is what I do best! It's what I learned doing Garry's show—comedy sketches. We can have a rep company like Garry's, and like *Caesar's Hour*. We can have guest stars! Music!"

Mike had other ideas. "Honey, we've got a great half-hour sitcom script that would fit you like a glove. It's called *Here's Agnes!* It's a sure thing!"

I handed the phone to Joe.

CBS scheduled the premiere of our show for Monday, September 11, 1967, opposite *I Spy* and *The Big Valley*, both of which had ratings in the top ten. Well, at least we'd have our thirty weeks until we had to find something else to do. In the meantime we could get rid of some orange crates and open up the packing boxes.

Joe flew to New York for a meeting with Mike. It was all very friendly, although Mike was clearly worried. There was a bulletin board mounted on the wall behind his desk, featuring the days of the week and the prime-time TV hours, with four-by-six-inch cards tacked on it, one for each CBS show in the fall lineup.

He had neglected to close the folding doors that would conceal the cards, so Joe saw our show on a card that read: "Sept.–Feb.: Burnett show." After February, the only thing in the slot was: "?" Obviously CBS thought we wouldn't last the whole season.

Actually, we didn't expect to last much longer, either.

Happily, though, we fooled both ourselves and CBS. We were to run for eleven wonderful seasons.

Our Rep Players

All the great comedy-variety shows that I watched in the early days of television had a repertoire of amazing comedians. *Your Show of Shows* starred Sid Caesar with Carl Reiner, Imogene Coca, and Howie Morris; *The Jackie Gleason Show* featured Art Carney and Audrey Meadows; *Caesar's Hour* included Nanette Fabray; and Garry Moore had his band of merry players. So when I set out to create my own variety show, it was only natural to try to follow in all those hallowed footsteps and put together a TV family of my own. And that's exactly what I did.

CLOCKWISE FROM LEFT: *Tim, Vicki, Harvey, and me.*

Vicki Lawrence

*

Our second baby was due in December 1966, and our show was scheduled to premiere in September 1967. One January afternoon I was tending to the mail at our desk. I looked and felt like I had swallowed a basketball. I was way overdue and a mite cranky, to say the least. I noticed an envelope that had been forwarded to me from CBS. It was about two or three weeks old. The letter was from a seventeen-year-old high school senior, asking for advice on how to get into show business. She said everyone told her she reminded them of me. She enclosed an article written about her from her local Inglewood, California, newspaper.

The accompanying photograph amazed me. This girl looked more like me at age seventeen than I did! Coincidentally, we had been toying with an idea of a recurring sketch in our show featuring a wife, a husband, and her kid sister. I couldn't help thinking that because of the resemblance this girl could be a likely candidate for the kid sister role. The interview in the paper went on about how talented she was, that she was a good student, and that she was a member of the Young Americans singing group. It also said that she was going to be a contestant in the annual Miss Fireball contest in Inglewood. I reread her letter. There was something about it that grabbed my attention—and gave me that funny feeling.

When I looked at the article again, I noticed that the date of the Miss Fireball event was that night. The article gave her parents' names. I picked up the telephone.

"Operator, do you have a listing for a Howard Lawrence in Inglewood?"

I dialed the number, and a woman answered.

"Hello?" Nice dulcet voice.

"Hello . . . is Vicki there?"

"This is her mother. May I say who's calling?" she asked softly.

"Hi, this is Carol Burnett. I just received—"

"VICKI!" A shout heard round the world. "*VICKI!*"

I heard whispering, a little shuffling, and then Vicki came on the line, her voice laced with ennui: "Oh, hi, Marsha."

I guess she and Marsha played telephone games.

After I finally convinced Vicki that I wasn't Marsha and she pulled herself together, I asked her if it would be okay if Joe and I came to the contest that night.

"We'll stand in the back after the lights go down. Are you happy with what you're performing?"

She was fine with all of it. I got the details of where and when, and hung up saying, "We'll see you tonight!"

I waddled into the kitchen, where Joe was eating a sandwich.

I said, "Don't get too comfortable. We're going to Inglewood tonight."

"We're what?"

"To catch the Miss Fireball contest at Hollywood Park. There's an auditorium there."

Calmly, he put down his sandwich. "Why?"

"I'm fourteen months pregnant, and I want to see the Miss Fireball contest."

"Are you nuts?"

I explained the whole thing to him, doing a show-and-tell with the letter and the article.

We went. Vicki did a comedy routine, accompanied herself on the guitar, and even played the kazoo. She also won the contest.

We congratulated her and went home.

My adorable basketball finally arrived January 18, 1967. Jody Hamilton, eight pounds, eleven ounces. I named her after Daddy.

Vicki paid us a visit in the hospital, bringing flowers. I thanked her and also told her we'd keep in touch, not saying anything about our show at that time.

A few months later, in the middle of casting our rep players, we were still up in the air about the "kid sister." We got in touch with Vicki and another young actress recommended by CBS, and decided to do a screen test. We wrote a sketch and taped it twice, once with Vicki and once with the other actress.

Perry Lafferty, a CBS executive, was a little worried about Vicki's being so wet behind the ears: "She's rough."

Our reply was, "So are diamonds, at first." She was hired.

Over the next eleven seasons, Vicki developed into an extraordinary comedienne, but at first it wasn't easy. She was only eighteen and unbelievably shy—so shy that she hardly ever spoke up in rehearsals unless someone spoke to her first. For the first couple of years she played my kid sister in an ongoing sketch called "Carol & Sis." I never really cared for this particular sketch (I thought it was bland), and beyond this Vicki wasn't being used much. Today, a network would tell us to let her go. CBS's Perry Lafferty trusted us, so she stayed.

Bless Harvey Korman. My beloved colleague took Vicki under his wing and helped her with character study, accents, voices—you name it. We started giving her more to do, and the more she did the better and more confident she became. (In the meantime "Carol & Sis" bit the dust, thank heavens.) Vicki was becoming a very good character actress with terrific comedy chops, so we gave her *lots* more to do.

Then along came Mama.

It was our seventh season and two of our best writers, Dick Clair and Jenna McMahon, came up with a sketch about a totally poor, ignorant, and dysfunctional family, consisting of Eunice (the wife), Ed (the husband), and Mama, Eunice's cranky mother. I loved it because it was all about character and situation, without any written jokes. In fact, if we had played it straight, there wouldn't have been many laughs; the sketch was more like a one-act play.

At first we thought I'd play Mama, but I leaned more toward Eunice (she reminded me of my own mother, who never saw her dreams realized). Harvey, of course, would be the hapless Ed. We thought of hiring an older actress to come in and play Mama, but Bob Mackie, our costumer, suggested Vicki. Why not give it a whirl? We sat down to read the script and I tore into Eunice with a kind of south Texas accent. I just saw these three people coming from that part of the country. It felt right. Harvey and Vicki followed suit with the accent, and the family was born.

Bob dressed Eunice in a godawful flowered print dress, white patent leather shoes, and a sad-looking dark brown wig that looked like it had been fried to death. Ed wore an old shirt and baggy mismatched pants with suspenders. Bob put Vicki in

Eunice and Mama going at it on The Carol Burnett Show.
COPYRIGHT © CBS PHOTO ARCHIVE/GETTY IMAGES

a padded dress, a gray wig, and spectacles. She wore no lipstick or eye makeup. She narrowed her eyes and jutted out her chin and laced into her character with a vengeance. She was hysterical. All our characters were way over the top, and the audience screamed with laughter.

"The Family" became a running feature of our show, airing

once every month or so; we wound up doing about thirty-five sketches before we went off the air. With each one Vicki got better and better. Here she had started out playing my kid sister and wound up brilliantly acting the part of Mama. I was incredibly proud when Vicki was awarded an Emmy in 1976. After our show she later starred in her own successful sitcom, *Mama's Family*.

Harvey Korman

*

By the time spring 1967 came around, Joe, as our producer (along with Bob Banner, executive producer), was busy putting together our writing and production staff, many of whom came out of Garry's show and were willing to take a chance on Hollywood. At the same time we were on the lookout for our very own gang of comedians who would play and have fun with us every week, the way we did on Garry's show.

Joe and I had been huge fans of *The Danny Kaye Show*, and particularly of his incredibly talented second banana, Harvey Korman. Harvey was to Danny what Carl Reiner was to Sid Caesar and Art Carney was to Jackie Gleason. "Second banana" is a term that has been used in comedy as far back as I can remember. It probably dates back to vaudeville. I never took to it much, though, because the good ones never fit into that "second" slot as far as I was concerned. In fact, lots of times they were the ones who walked away with the laughs . . . if the star would allow it. Those stars I've mentioned weren't afraid to let their

The fabulous duo: Tim Conway and Harvey Korman.

teammates score a touchdown. They knew it only made the show better overall.

Danny Kaye's show went off the air in 1967 and we were premiering that fall. All I could think was, *We need a Harvey Korman.* We needed a consummate actor with comedy chops to spare. The penny finally dropped, the lightbulb lit up, and I came to the brilliant conclusion to actually ask THE Harvey Korman himself if he would work with us. Now that Danny's show would no longer be on, could we . . . would he . . . ?

I believe we had a call in to his agent when one afternoon I happened to see Harvey himself headed for his car in the CBS parking lot at Television City. He didn't notice me. I thought about it for a nanosecond and then I shouted, "Harvey!"

He turned and smiled. We hardly knew each other. I waved, smiled back, and then proceeded to jump him. I may be exaggerating, but I seem to remember leaning him back over a car hood.

"Please, *please* be on our show! You're the very best! PLEASE?"

It wasn't exactly the most professional way to offer someone a job, but it worked. Harvey signed on, and I was in heaven.

As I write this, I'm fairly sure that somewhere there must be someone who is as brilliant a comedic actor as Harvey (who, week after week, created hysterically funny characters with different accents and looks, in only four days of rehearsal), but I don't think there's anybody who can *top* what he could do. I've always felt that it's a wise thing to play tennis with a better player, because it makes your own game that much better. And that's what Harvey was to me as a fellow actor. He made my game better. He made *everyone's* game better.

And then one Friday night after a show I fired him.

It went like this.

* * *

Friday A.M. We were working on a rock 'n' roll finale. It was a large set and because it would take too much time to get it together for our evening audience we would, at times like this, pre-tape the finale and then play it back on the TV monitors for the studio audience later. Our guests that week were Tim Conway and Petula Clark, two of the nicest people in the world. We were all in costume, dancing and lip-syncing to our pre-recorded voices.

Now, at times Harvey could get into a mood. This morning, in his Elvis getup, he was definitely not a happy camper. I'd always ignore him whenever he got like that, because the next thing you knew he would turn on a dime and go back to being his hysterically funny and loveable self. But not *this* morning. I could practically see the black cloud hovering over his head. He was actually *scowling.* As far as I was concerned, he could scowl at me till the cows came home, but this time he scowled at our guests and was short with them.

After the taping, when everyone was changing for our camera run-through, I went to Harvey's dressing room and knocked on the door. He was still scowling when he opened it. I asked him what was wrong, but he was in no mood to discuss it, intimating that it was none of my business. I told him it *was* my business when it affected the show and our guests. He could be rude to *me*, but not to our guests! Whereupon he told me I couldn't dictate to him how to feel or act, and as far as he was concerned he'd just as soon go home and never come back after tonight's show. He closed the door.

Stunned, I didn't know what to do. I felt that this was in my lap and I didn't want anyone else to know just yet what had happened, not even Joe. I had never been confrontational before—it's just not in my makeup—but in this case I knew I had to be. So what did I do? I conjured up a character to play, a cross between Barbara Stanwyck and Joan Crawford, women who weren't afraid to speak up and be strong. Acting like them would give me the courage to stand up to Harvey.

Okay. It was time to take the stage.

* * *

Friday, lunch break. In my dressing room, I called Harvey's agent, Tony Fantozzi.

TONY: Hey, Carol! What's up?

ME: Harvey's off the show after tonight.

TONY: Whaa . . . ?

ME: He wants off the show, so I'm granting his wish.

TONY: What're ya talkin' about? Does Joe know about this?

ME: Not yet. He's in the director's booth. I'll tell him after the show, but it won't matter what anybody says or thinks. Harvey's off the show.

TONY: What about his contract?

ME: If he wants off, I want him off. If there's a problem, I'll go to the union.

TONY: Jeez . . . what did he do?

ME: Tony, I don't mind when he gets into one of his moods, but when he's rude to our guests, I'm not gonna put up with it! I mean, how on earth can you be mean to Petula Clark and Tim Conway? It boggles the mind!

TONY: Have you told Harvey?

ME: After we get through the show tonight.

TONY: Jeez . . .

We got through the show that night. I don't think anybody sensed the tension between Harvey and me. He was his usual professional self, but I was a total wreck.

* * *

Friday, after the show. I knock on Harvey's dressing room door.

HARVEY: Come in.

He's sitting at his makeup table. I sit down and look at him in the mirror.

ME: Well, you've got your wish.
HARVEY: What're you talking about?

He turns around to face me.

ME: You don't have to come back anymore if you're
          that unhappy. I called your agent and he's aware
          of the situation.
HARVEY: You called Fantozzi?
ME: Yep.
HARVEY: Well . . . I have a contract. . . .
ME: That can be taken care of. You were rude to our
          guests and because of your behavior I was
          screwing up all over the place tonight during
          the show. I can't work like that, so if you want
          off, you're free to go.

I head for the door. He stops me.

ME: What?
HARVEY: What can I do?
ME: You asking for a reprieve?
HARVEY: Sort of. Well, yes.

ME: *(pause)* Okay, here's what we do. This coming
        Monday, I want to see you *cheerful.*

He nods.

ME: Not only Monday, but the whole week! And
        you're never, *ever* to be nasty to one of our
        guests or anyone on our crew. We all have
        moods, but we don't bring them to work. Okay?

He nods again.

ME: In fact, it would tickle me pink to hear you
        whistling in the hall!

We shake hands.

HARVEY: See you Monday.

On the way home in the car, I told Joe what I'd done. He
couldn't stop laughing. He was proud of me, but he got a special
kick out of how I willed myself to be a combination of Stanwyck
and Crawford in order to face Harvey.

Monday morning I was in my office, waiting for the gang
and our guests to show up for the first reading of the week's
script. Vicki and Lyle got there first. I decided to go down the
hall to the ladies' room before everyone else arrived. As I was on
the way back to my office, the elevator door opened and Harvey
stepped out. We both froze for a split second. Then he started
skipping, dancing, and *whistling* his way down the hall to my
office! I doubled over with laughter.

Later that day, I heard from some of the crew that after our little chat Friday night, Harvey went across the street to the local watering hole, where a lot of the gang went to have a drink or two (or three) after the show, and proceeded to stand on top of the bar and tell everyone what had happened.

He then lifted his glass and toasted me!

The following week we had a plaque put on his dressing room door:

MR. HAPPY-GO-LUCKY

For some perverse reason, Harvey always got a kick out of telling the story about the night he got fired.

* * *

After our show went off the air, Harvey and I were never parted for long. Joe and I enjoyed countless dinners with Harvey and his wife, Debby, and Tim Conway and his wife, Sharkey, at our favorite restaurants. I used to kid that it was dangerous to eat with that group; we would laugh so hard that someone needed to be ready to perform the Heimlich maneuver!

Harvey took ill just before Christmas of 2007. He fought long and hard through several operations, and often we thought he would pull through. The doctors were amazed at his resilience. But he finally succumbed in May 2008, with Debby and his family at his side.

I will love Mr. Happy-Go-Lucky and hold him in my heart forever.

Lyle Waggoner

*

In the mid-sixties I was still relying on the goofy, zany, loudmouthed, ugly-duckling caricature that had worked so well for me during the Garry Moore years and as the man-hungry princess in *Once upon a Mattress*. So it made sense to cast an unbelievably handsome announcer for me to fawn and make goo-goo eyes over. I remembered Jack Benny with his announcer, Don Wilson. This was different, but it had the same premise: *Have fun with the announcer. Make him a character in the show, not just a commercial-pusher.*

We held auditions. I have never seen so many gorgeous men in one room in my life. In walked Lyle Waggoner. Gorgeous? Yes. But so much more. He was incredibly funny. He had a sly, tongue-in-cheek delivery that told you he was putting himself on and not taking himself seriously. No question, he was the one. Later, during our long run with the show, we started giving Lyle roles in the sketches because we trusted his comedic instincts. We weren't wrong. He was very funny doing various characters and wound up playing a much bigger role in the show than just the announcer. After a while, we squelched the idea of my fawning and making goo-goo eyes at him. Lyle had become much more than a foil for me. He had become a true rep player.

Lyle also had other talents. After we first went on the air, he was getting piles of fan mail from swooning girls all over the country. He acquired a card table and a chair, which he set up in the reception area outside the writers' rooms as his "office." When we were on a break he would head for his card table and answer his mail. About a month or two later, I walked by and he was opening several envelopes, taking out the cash inside, and stacking it neatly on the card table. I asked him what was going on and he showed me a very professional brochure with his photograph on the cover, entitled *How to Audition and Get the Job*. He had put together advice for would-be actors and performers— for a dollar a pop!

I read the brochure, which turned out to be very well written and, in my view, a great value at a dollar. But it gave me new insight into my multi-talented colleague: Lyle was quite the entrepreneur!

Lyle was also a talented carpenter. One week Tim and I were doing a sketch about a nerdy couple that meets on a cruise ship. The ship, built by our set designer Paul Barnes, took up the entire stage. It was designed to rock back and forth, enabling Tim and me to slide up and down the deck, hanging on for dear life.

During rehearsals Lyle asked Paul what he was going to do with the set after the show was over. Paul told him it was too big to store, so it would be cut up and burned. Lyle asked if he could take it home. No problem. After the show, the crew took the set apart and Lyle hauled it home in a huge pickup truck.

A few weeks later, a bunch of us went to a party at the Waggoners' house. Lyle and his beautiful wife, Sharon, were showing

Lyle: a guy to swoon over!

us around, and took us into a small, cozy, nicely furnished room. Lyle smiled. "Recognize anything?"

I didn't.

"It's the cruise ship set. I used the wood and built another room!"

Today, Lyle has a hugely successful business furnishing

movie studios with his "Star Waggons" (motor homes), which house actors working on films and/or television shoots. I've been in a few of his motor homes and they're definitely the best.

No question about it. He's a man of all trades.

Smart, funny, and as gorgeous as ever, silver hair and all.

Tim Conway

*

ecause he was so essential to our show, people assume that Tim Conway was in on it from the get-go. Not so. He was a regular guest (one or two times a month) until the ninth year, when (DUH! How stupid were we?) we finally asked him to be on every single week. Tim was a true original, with a comedic mind so brilliant that it's downright scary. His sketches with Harvey Korman deserve a spot in whatever cultural time capsule we're setting aside for future generations.

We always taped two shows on Fridays with two different audiences. The early show was a dress rehearsal that we taped as a backup. Tim would do the first show as written, "to the ink." Then, as we were getting ready for the next show, he would check in with our director, Dave Powers: "You get all the shots?"

Dave would respond, "Yes." (He always got all the shots.)

Tim would then ask Dave to change some things for the second show. For instance: "Instead of shooting a close-up of me when I go to the window, could you make it a head-to-toe shot?"

This meant that Tim had come up with some outrageous

103

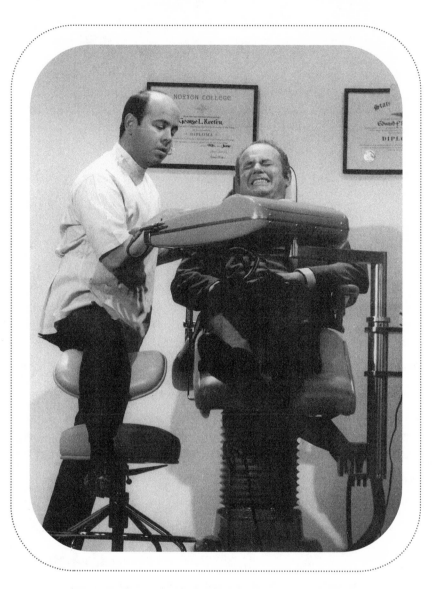

Tim and poor, helpless Harvey in the dentist sketch.

bit of business that we hadn't seen or planned for. Now the fun would begin. Whatever Tim had been secretly cooking up all week blossomed into sheer hysterics in the second show, with Dave and the camera crew winging it right alongside him. Ninety-nine percent of the time we aired the second taping with all of Tim's ad-libs and improvisations because they were so much funnier than the "ink" that we'd planned.

Tim's dentist sketch with Harvey has to go down in television history as one of the funniest bits ever. Tim played the dentist, fresh out of school, and Harvey was his very first patient. The meat of the sketch was that Tim kept accidentally shooting himself with novocaine, first in his hand, then in his leg, and finally winding up with the needle between his eyebrows. As usual, he came up with most of these bits himself, and we all saw them for the first time in the second show.

I was screaming with laughter watching the monitor in my dressing room, so I ran out to the backstage area and watched from the wings. The entire audience was exploding. Our cameramen couldn't contain themselves, either. There wasn't a dry eye (or seat) in the house. And then I looked at Harvey. He couldn't move from his chair. Utterly helpless with laughter. He tried his best to keep it together, but it was no use. Tears were spurting out of his eyes. Tim was relentless.

Tim didn't just improvise; he also wrote a lot of the sketches we did. Mr. Tudball and Mrs. Wiggins were his creations, for instance. We trusted his instincts, and we were never wrong.

Tim Conway is fearless in his comedy. If the audience doesn't get it at first, he keeps on keeping on until they do. Unfortunately, our show has been accused of showing actors cracking up at times, breaking character. Guilty as charged. But it was never unwarranted. I dare anyone to be on camera and to keep it together when Conway gets on a roll. We really tried very hard *not* to break up, but when we did, it was honest.

People often ask me what Tim is like in "real life." First of all, he's one of the sweetest and most thoughtful people I've ever known. That said, he's also nuts.

One night Joe and I went to a party in the Valley given by our voice-over announcer, Ernie Anderson, and his wife, Edwinna. The whole gang was there: a bunch of our writers, some of the dancers, and of course Tim and Harvey. When we arrived, there was Tim, sitting on the couch holding a conversation with somebody, his entire head wrapped in toilet paper but for two eyeholes and an opening for his mouth. No, he wasn't drunk. His head was simply swathed in toilet paper. I don't know how or why the bit got started, but there he was, looking like Claude Rains in *The Invisible Man*.

He stayed that way the entire evening. After a while, nobody seemed to notice. Our host took a Polaroid of Tim's face, and it came out the size of a driver's license picture. Tim trimmed the photo, took out his wallet, and inserted the Polaroid over his regular driver's license picture. (No laminated licenses in those days.) The party ended, and as Joe and I were driving away, we saw Tim get in his car, still looking like the Invisible Man.

What happened next? There are some nice quiet streets in the San Fernando Valley, and Tim, after leaving the party, drove home on one particular street where he knew there was always a cop car lying in wait at a four-way stop sign. Tim purposely didn't come to a complete stop at the sign. He heard the siren and saw the red light in his rearview mirror. Pulling over to the side of the road, he stopped, rolled down his window, and waited for the policeman, his face still wrapped in the toilet paper.

The policeman looked at Tim and asked for his license. Tim handed it over.

The comedy gods were smiling that night. The cop had a sense of humor.

Conway's Cancellation

✳

Tim had had several shows of his own before he came to us. They never lasted more than thirteen weeks, which was why his vanity license plates read "13 WKS." He liked to tell us about the time he was cancelled by ABC when he was the star of *Rango*, a sitcom about an inept cowboy in the Old West. While Tim was always hysterically funny, the *Rango* scripts left a lot to be desired, plus the show wasn't shot before an audience. It was filmed like a movie—a big mistake because Tim shines before an audience, ad-libbing and improvising. The show had been on the air a few short weeks when there was a knock on Tim's dressing room door.

TIM: *(changing his boots for the upcoming scene)*
          Come in.
(Enter a nervous-looking young man in a suit and tie, repre-senting the network. He reminded Tim of Don Knotts.)
THE SUIT: Mr. C-C-Conway?
TIM: *(mid-boot)* Hi.

THE SUIT: M-Mr. Conway . . . hi . . . er . . . um . . . I'm
Albert Tart from ABC.

TIM: *(friendly, sensing that this suit was somewhat of
an underling at the network)* Well, hi there,
Albert, come on in. Make yourself
comfortable. What can I do for you?

What came out of poor, nervous Albert's mouth next is probably the oddest (and funniest) cancellation speech of all time.

THE SUIT: Stop doing this.

Tim never made it to the other boot.

Australia

*

In the fall of 1973 our show was tapped to be the first television show to open the newly finished Sydney Opera House. We were thrilled, and gathered the necessary crew for the trip: Joe as our producer; our director, Dave Powers; our lead dancer, Don Crichton; our choreographer, Ernie Flatt; a couple of writers; and of course Harvey, Tim, and Vicki, along with the brilliant ballet artist Edward Villella as our guest.

The show consisted of a musical opening with the dancers performing a number outside on the steps of the opera house to the tune of "Waltzing Matilda." Harvey, Vicki, and I would do sketches, and Tim, as the world's oldest maestro, would conduct the symphony orchestra to the tune of the *William Tell Overture.* Edward Villella had a solo turn, and our finale was to be a fractured version of *Swan Lake*, featuring Edward as the hero and me dancing with him as the Charwoman. We all stayed at the same hotel, which featured a breathtaking view of the harbor and the opera house.

Rehearsals began, and at the beginning everyone would get

together in the evening to sample the various restaurants around town. After a few days, however, our group began to shrink as people somewhat mysteriously split off; liaisons were forming, which was typical of working on location. Major and mini love affairs were popping up all over the place. I guess being halfway around the world tempted some people to throw caution to the wind. Naturally each couple thought their tryst was a big secret. Nope. Things like that have a way of getting out, but we all did our best to keep mum. Joe and I felt a bit weird about all the goings-on, but these were all adults and it was none of our business.

One night, shortly before we were to do the show, Joe and I made a date to have dinner with Tim, who was traveling solo. We called his suite, and he suggested we come by to pick him up.

After we got off the elevator, we went to his suite and knocked.

"Come on in."

We opened the unlocked door and entered the living room. No Tim.

He called out from the bedroom, "In here. C'mon in."

We hesitantly approached the open door and peered into the dimly lit room.

There was Tim, bare-chested in bed, covers up to his waist, smoking a cigarette with his arm around a sheep, whose head was peeking out from underneath the comforter.

"Hi, guys. Be right with you." Getting up, he kissed his bed partner, patted her on the head, and said, "Don't wait up, Barbara. I'll see you in the morning."

Then he looked at us and winked. "I know you'll keep this to yourselves."

Joe and I collapsed with laughter. "Barbara" was an unbelievably realistic life-sized toy sheep Tim had bought in the gift shop.

None of us opted for lamb chops that night.

Bob Mackie

*

W hat can you say about a man who, for eleven years, designed as many as fifty costumes a week for our variety show?

Plenty.

When we were putting the staff together in 1967, we knew that for our show costume design would be as important as writing. It's a huge job. On a comedy-variety show the designer has to create looks for every character in every sketch and musical number, both silly and serious.

Joe and I had watched the *Alice in Wonderland* special on TV and had also seen Mitzi Gaynor's show, and in both cases we marveled at the outfits. They were gloriously clever. We noted the name Bob Mackie in the credits, called him, and made a date for him to come to our house for a meeting. At the appointed hour the doorbell rang and I opened the door to find a very handsome young boy (he looked to be about twelve) claiming to be Bob Mackie.

It turned out he was. (And he was in his early twenties.) We talked for a bit about what we were looking for. He was charming and funny and offered several clever ideas, so he was hired on the spot.

It was the beginning of a beautiful relationship that lasts to this day. Bob saved many a comedy sketch on our show with his wit and sharp eye for detail. I trusted his judgment so much that after the third week I stopped asking to see his drawings of the characters I'd be playing. Often he'd surprise me, and I'd always be delighted.

On Fridays we would give Bob the script for the following week's show, and he would begin to design every single outfit worn by our regular cast, including our dancers and singers, plus our guest stars. He even designed the wigs, and many times the makeup, for the various characters we played—sometimes fifty outfits total—and he did all this in less than a week! To this day, I don't know how he did it.

My costume-fitting day was Wednesday, and I couldn't wait for that morning, when I'd head to his workplace to see what he had come up with. There were times when I didn't have a clue about how I was going to play a character until I put on the outfit Bob had cooked up for me. For instance, the character of Mrs. Wiggins had originally been written as a somewhat doddering old lady. Bob changed all that. When I arrived for my weekly fitting, I looked at the drawing he had made and there was this buxom blonde with a flowered blouse, tight black skirt, stiletto heels, and long red fingernails. Instead of seeing her as ancient, he suggested I play her as a bimbo—someone the "IQ fairy never visited." I loved the idea.

I got into the outfit, and he stuck a blond wig on my head. The skinny black skirt was very tight around my knees but baggy in the behind.

The dress!

ME: Bob, I think we're going to have to take in the rear so it'll fit.

BOB: Why don't you stick out your butt to make it fit?

I did, and that's how the "Wiggins walk" was born. I had found my character.

Then there was the Wednesday when I went in for the *Gone With the Wind* fitting. Our takeoff was called "Went With the Wind," and I was playing Starlett O'Hara. It was a brilliant send-up of the movie, with Harvey playing Rat Butler. There's a classic scene in the movie when Scarlett takes the green velvet draperies with the golden tie tassels down from the window and has Mammy make a dress for her so that she can impress Rhett. In our written version, when Rat is waiting at the bottom of the stairs for Starlett's entrance, I was to appear at the top of the stairs with the draperies simply hanging there on my body as I descended to greet Rat Butler.

Funny enough. It was sure to get a good laugh.

However, when I walked into the fitting room Bob said, "I have an idea for the drapery bit."

He then brought out THE DRESS. It was a green velvet gown *still attached to the curtain rod* that would fit across my shoulders, with golden curtain tassels tied at the waist. He had even made a hat out of the rest of the tassels.

I fell on the floor.

That Friday taping will go down in history. When Starlett appeared at the top of the stairs in that getup, the audience went crazy. It has been called one of the funniest moments in the history of television comedy.

And it was all because of Bob.

Today his spectacular creation is on view at the Smithsonian.

Jim Nabors

*

I remember watching an episode of *Gomer Pyle* where Gomer, played by Jim Nabors, sits on a porch swing with his girlfriend and sings a beautiful folk song, accompanying himself on the guitar. I thought he was wonderful, and sent him a fan letter telling him so. It was 1965. We met shortly after that when Jim was in New York on business, and we hit it off immediately.

After Joe and I moved to California, we got together often with Jim, and I thought of him as the brother I never had. When I gave birth to Jody, Jim Nabors became her godfather.

Jim bought a home in Hawaii and lived a double life as a farmer in Maui. I remember performing with Jim one night at the MGM Grand in Las Vegas. Having just come offstage after doing his encore of "Impossible Dream" to a standing ovation, he looked at me waiting in the wings and said in his Gomer Pyle voice, "Well, I just bought me another tractor!"

When my variety show was about to premiere, Jim was our very first guest. When the show took off we looked on Jim as

Jim and me rehearsing for The Carol Burnett Show.

our good-luck charm, so he wound up being the guest on our first show every season for eleven years.

Jim is still living in Hawaii. We don't see each other as much as we'd like to, but we call each other often and play catch-up. And Jim, I just want you to know that I love my good-luck charm very much.

Talking to the Audience

✳

Now that we had put together our cast, Joe went about the business of hiring staff: writers, choreographer, set designer, and so on. Many of our first choices had worked on *The Garry Moore Show* in New York and, happily for us, were willing to take the chance and move out to California to be on our show. Arnie Rosen came on board as our talented head comedy writer. The extraordinarily versatile Ernie Flatt signed on as choreographer. Bob Wright came to us as associate producer. Several of Garry's original dancers and singers joined us, including our brilliant lead dancer, Don Crichton, plus two of our best production assistants, known to all as Sharkey and Mumpsy. When the hiring was complete and we all got together, it felt like a class reunion.

One night Joe, Bob Banner (our co-executive producer), and I were at dinner kicking around some ideas. We were premiering in a few short weeks. We knew we wanted comedy sketches, music, dancing and singing, and guest stars each week. We also hoped to develop returning characters, like Jackie Gleason's Poor

Soul and Ralph Kramden, Sid Caesar's German Professor, and Red Skelton's Clem Kadiddlehopper.

Bob brought up the subject of how we would open the show. It was, and still is, typical to have a warm-up comedian come out before the taping and tell jokes to get the audience in a happy and anticipatory mood. Garry Moore never used that approach. He was his own warm-up man. He would go out onstage before the cameras rolled and kid around with the audience by doing a question-and-answer session. Every week I stood in the wings listening to his give-and-take with the audience. Garry was amazingly quick. He was always funny, always accessible, and always warm. His approach was a great way to get everyone in the audience in the mood for the taping. Also, this way they felt they really knew him.

Bob suggested that I do the same thing, except that we'd actually tape these audience chats to show on the air. I balked at the idea, big-time. First of all, I didn't have the confidence to think that I could come up with anything interesting off the cuff, and I didn't want any planted questions. All I could think of was that Garry's sessions were completely improvised. They were honest.

At least we knew how we would close the show. The cast and guest stars would all line up for a bow, and I would ask the guests to sign my autograph book. Joe, who had been a songwriter and musician before turning producer, wrote our theme song, "I'm So Glad We Had This Time Together," which I would sing. Then I'd tug on my ear for Nanny, and we'd all wave goodnight.

Bob kept pressing me about opening the show by doing Q & A's with our studio audience, saying how important it was for me to be myself before we jumped into the sketches and various characters for the rest of the hour. I finally (and very reluctantly) gave in. I agreed to try it a couple of times, and if it didn't work, we'd forget about it forever.

I remember coming out onstage before that first show, absolutely terrified, and looking at all the folks in their seats waiting for me to say something. What if no one had a question? Or worse, what if someone *did*, and I didn't have an answer?

"Hi, and welcome to our show. Um . . . let's see if you have anything to say . . . I mean, if you have any questions . . . about our show . . . or whatever. Let's bump up the lights!"

The lights went up. The audience was staring at me politely.

"Anything at all? Just raise your hands."

No hands.

"I mean, whatever you have in mind . . . Anything?"

The flop sweat began to roll down the back of my neck.

FINALLY, a hand shot up. "Yes?"

The man asked, "Who's on?"

I talked about Harvey, Vicki, and Lyle. Then I announced that Jim Nabors, my buddy and the godfather of my daughter Jody, was our premiere guest star. Jim was one of the most popular performers in the country, and the audience went wild. They were warming up, and I was breathing easier.

We tried the opening again the following week, and it went a little better. By the third week I was beginning to have fun, and the audience, having seen the first two airings, knew what to expect and weren't as shy about raising their hands. And the questions got funnier.

ME: *(pointing to a raised hand)* Yes, the lady in the pink.

Q: What has been your most embarrassing question?

ME: *(thinking for a moment)* I think my most embarrassing question was whether or not I'd had a sex change. *(Laughter)* Yep, I think that takes the cake. *(Pointing to another audience member)* Yes?

Q: Did you? *(Much laughter)*

Next question . . .

Q: Did you ever take acting lessons?
ME: Yes, I did . . . when I was at UCLA, I studied for a while.
Q: Think it did you any good?

Another time a woman raised her hand, stood up, and asked if she could come up onstage and sing a song. She was dressed somewhat like Bea Arthur playing Maude, and there was a physical resemblance to boot. I said, "Sure, fine," and she shot up to the stage like the Road Runner. Before I even finished asking what she'd like to sing, she turned to the orchestra and yelled out, "'YOU MADE ME LOVE YOU' IN THE KEY OF G!"

When the audience screamed with laughter, she shushed them and proceeded to belt it out, and I mean BELT! She was fearless, and I might add she was pretty good, too. After she got through the first couple of bars I decided to join her, and the solo became a duet. We were both belting it out in harmony, wailing away, and the audience was clapping to the rhythm. It was going beautifully and we were having a lot of fun. Then we came to the ending. I had in mind one way to vocally end the number, and she had a different take on how we should wind it up. So after a great beginning and middle, our ending left a lot to be desired. What had started out as a dynamic duet was now pitifully petering out. She shot a look at me and, obviously pissed, said, "YOU SCREWED IT UP!" The audience ate her up, and as far as I was concerned, she was pure gold.

Another one of my favorite moments happened when a lady in the audience asked me when I was going to do another takeoff on Shirley Temple. We had done a couple of short bits earlier in the season where I played Shirley Dimple being interviewed by

Harvey, who was playing a newsman. Upon hearing the question from the lady in the audience, the crew and cameramen burst out laughing.

Why? *Because in that very show, that very night, we were doing a complete twenty-five-minute send-up of a Shirley Temple movie that we had been rehearsing all week as our big extravaganza finale, taking up the entire second half of the hour!* It consisted of four elaborate sets and dozens of costumes, with original music and lyrics by Ken and Mitzie Welch, backed by our regular twenty-eight-piece orchestra, led by Peter Matz, plus guest stars Anthony Newley and Bernadette Peters, along with Harvey, Vicki, Lyle, and our dancers.

And this was a total and complete coincidence!

Instead of explaining this to the lady and the audience, I decided to have some fun with her. I asked, "Do you like it when we do Shirley?" She smiled and nodded. I went on, "Gosh, I'm not sure, but maybe we can whip up *something* before the end of the show. I can't promise you, but we'll try."

The first half of the show featured solos by Anthony Newley and Bernadette Peters, and a couple of sketches. Then we came to the second half.

First came the overture, with Lyle's announcement: "Ladies and gentlemen! Tonight we present our movie of the week, LITTLE MISS SHOWBIZ! Starring Shirley Dimple!"

The first scene finds Shirley in an orphanage with other little girls in matching PJs singing and dancing on and around their beds in tap shoes. The story revolves around Shirley and her two uncles: Uncle Meany (Harvey) is a rich Scrooge type, and his out-of-work younger brother, Uncle Miney (Anthony Newley), wants to write a successful Broadway show starring his girlfriend (Bernadette Peters). Both uncles want to adopt Shirley, whose father, Moe, died in an accident. Uncle Meany wins custody because he's so awfully rich. Shirley sings a goodbye song to her fellow orphanage mates and sadly leaves with the wealthy and unpleasant Uncle Meany, much to the sorrow of Uncle Miney, who sings a sad lament with the remaining orphans.

We next find Uncle Miney in his cold-water flat with his girlfriend, trying to write a hit show tune, which they sing while the girlfriend taps her way around the room. After the number, Shirley bursts into the flat, having run away from Meany, and begs her kind but poor uncle Miney to let her stay with him. The girlfriend isn't too happy with this arrangement because she thinks Shirley's a brat. Shirley's not too crazy about the girlfriend either, and tries to come between her and Miney by writing and singing her own hit song for Broadway, which Uncle Miney flips over, claiming that they'll have a major hit with that song starring Shirley. After they finish singing it together, Uncle Meany bangs down the door demanding that Shirley come back with him. They agree to take this problem to the highest court in the land.

Our next scene finds us in a courtroom with a jury, where Shirley's fate is to be determined. On hand are the two uncles and the girlfriend. Shirley enters and sings to the judge, segueing into sitting on Uncle Meany's lap and singing to him, asking him not to be so mean. His heart is touched, and Uncle Miney jumps up and asks Shirley to sing and tap-dance for the court.

She takes off her coat and reveals a sequined costume with dozens of petticoats. As this is happening, the set revolves, the jury members and the judge remove their outer garments, becoming dancers and singers, and lo and behold, we find ourselves in a Broadway show with everybody singing and tapping their hearts out, including Uncle Meany, who by now has decided to invest in Uncle Miney and Shirley's show.

TA-DA! The end.

Just before the cast took its bows, I asked the lady in the audience how she liked the show.

She said, "Oh, thank you so much for going to all that trouble!"

* * *

And so it went, for eleven wonderful years. The Q & A became one of my favorite parts of the show. Because it wasn't scripted, anything could happen—and it usually did!

The Writers' Room

*

W e had several comedy writers on our show working in offices right across the hall from mine,
including our head writer, Arnie Rosen, who had
been a writer on Garry Moore's show and had moved out to
California to run our comedy staff. We were delighted to have
him at the helm; Arnie had a sense of humor to be envied.

During our lunch break he and the rest of the writers
would often watch comedy shows that had been off the air for
years, starring the all-time greats, some of whom had given
these writers their first jobs: Milton Berle, Sid Caesar, Jackie
Gleason, and many others. Sometimes I would go into the dark
screening room to watch for a few minutes and laugh along with
the gang.

One day I went across the hall to ask Arnie a question
about a particular sketch we were doing that week. He was in the
screening room with the rest of the staff. Without looking at the
screen, I went over to Arnie's chair and bent over to whisper my
question so as not to disturb anyone. I heard a couple of long,

drawn-out moans, and turned around to see where they were coming from. I had never seen a porn film in my life, and my jaw dropped to the floor. I had been set up—beautifully.

I sputtered: "Ohhh! Omigod! Th-That's the worst thing I've ever SEEN!"

Arnie calmly replied, "Well, gosh, Carol, he's doing the best he can."

Cary Grant

※

We were in the rehearsal hall getting ready to read the week's script.

"Cary Grant?"

Harvey grinned and nodded.

"CARY Grant?"

More grinning and more nodding from Harvey.

"*THE* CARY GRANT?"

Harvey's head was bobbing up and down so hard I thought it would fall off his neck.

"How? When?"

We were gathered around the big table for our regular Monday morning reading of that week's show. Vicki, Tim, Lyle, the guests (I don't remember who), our director, Dave Powers, and I were all glued to Harvey's story about the weekend party he had attended in Beverly Hills.

"Okay, it was Saturday night, and HE was there! Naturally, he was gorgeous, charming, funny, and—get this—interested in *me*! He *never misses* our show! In fact, he asked the hostess if she'd mind if he disappeared for an hour at ten o'clock because we were on that night."

I tried catching my breath. "Omigod, you mean Cary Grant actually knows who we are?"

"He went on and on about the show and how much we make him laugh."

All of us were silent for a bit.

Cary Grant. I remembered going to his movies when I was growing up, and Nanny saying, "He's the second most beautiful thing in the world next to Hedy Lamarr." I thought he was beautiful, too, but I also thought he was funny. He could do great body-pounding pratfalls. He was a fantastic athlete. Charm, of course, oozed out of his every pore. By this time our variety show had already been on the air a few years, and I had had the thrill of meeting and working with—dare I say it—icons. However, a handful of stars go beyond even that iconic thing. They work in the stratosphere, they're one of a kind; never again will we see their like. And Cary Grant is on that short list. I couldn't shake off the wonderment I felt knowing that *he* knew who *I* was, and he was a fan to boot. The idea was overwhelming.

A few weeks later, Joe and I were invited to a cocktail party at Peggy Lee's house in Beverly Hills. One of the greatest pop singers ever, she had been a guest on our show a few times, and we'd grown pretty friendly. We were the first ones to show up. My fault—I could never stand being late to anything. Our coats were hung up in the hall closet and I began making friends with the caterer.

It wasn't long before Peggy Lee appeared, looking beautiful in an elegant hostess gown. In a few minutes the doorbell started ringing in earnest, and it wasn't long before the place was wall-to-wall with celebrities. The party was in full swing— Alan King putting everyone in stitches, hors d'oeuvres being cleaned off the trays before they made it across the room, Frank

My awkward meeting with Cary Grant
(with Peggy Lee and Joe in the background).
COURTESY OF CAROL BURNETT

Sinatra's "Come Fly with Me" swinging through the speakers. And then . . . suddenly, the whole party quieted down, and all heads turned to the front door. I followed suit.

Cary Grant.

Peggy went over to greet him. Taking his elbow, she walked him into the room, and people stepped aside for them. She introduced him to those who had never had the honor, while even the biggest stars all but genuflected. He was very much at ease, laughing and shaking hands, and as they got nearer I bolted for the coat closet.

Joe was at my heels. "What're you doing? Don't you want to meet Cary Grant?"

"No." *My coat . . . my coat. Here it is, the short beige number. Please, God, get me outta here.*

Joe couldn't believe it. "Are you nuts? All you've been talking about is Harvey's story of meeting him, and here he is! Here's your chance!"

I had one sleeve on. "Let's go."

"Will you please tell me what the hell's the matter with you?"

Poor Joe—he just didn't get it.

I tried to explain. "Joe, you just don't get it. Look, he *likes* me! He makes it a point to watch our show every single week! Now, do you think I want to *spoil* that?"

"Why would you spoil it?"

I had always thought Joe was smarter than that.

"Because I wouldn't know what to say or how to act, and I would make a fool of myself, and he wouldn't like me anymore! Okay? Got it? Let's go!"

We headed for the front door. The knob was within reach when I felt a tap on my shoulder. I turned around and there they were, Peggy and HIM.

"Carol, where're you goin'?" Peggy asked. "You can't leave yet! Cary's dying to meet you! Cary, meet Carol and Joe Hamilton. Joe produces Carol's show." He and Joe shook hands, and then his attention turned to me.

Oh, gee. I looked up into his face, *that* face, and I forced a lame smile. He took my hand and his mouth started moving . . . and I couldn't *hear* him! My heartbeat was so loud that I thought my ears were going to explode. Watching his lips move, I just knew that whatever he was saying had to be the most charming words anyone had ever uttered, but I couldn't *hear*!

He kept on and on, holding my hand, sometimes even squeezing it a little. I thought he'd never stop. But then he did. His mouth had stopped moving. Silence. *Oh God, it's my turn now. He's waiting for me to say something . . . anything.*

Then I opened my mouth, and out it came in a rush. "You're a credit to your profession."

Why didn't the floor open up? Why hadn't we made it to the door in time?

Why did Peggy Lee have to be so sweet?

Why was I born?

On the way home in the car, Joe looked over at me, smiled sweetly, patted my knee, winked, and said, "Sweetheart, I'll never doubt you again."

That, at least, got a chuckle out of me.

*With Cary at the track: I'm much more
comfortable with him here!*

Cary, Harvey, and Tim
at the Racetrack

*

I t wasn't long after my first disastrous meeting with Cary
Grant that we actually became friends by way of attending
parties and various fund-raising events in town. He had a
private box at the racetrack, and one Wednesday he called and
invited Joe and me to join him and his lovely wife, Barbara, for a
Saturday outing.

That Saturday was a pretty exciting event for us. Cary and
Barbara were great hosts and made us feel right at home. We
went to the track a few more times, and even though we weren't
into the ponies that much, we always had a lot of fun. Let me put
it this way: if you didn't know Cary Grant was a movie star icon,
you never would have guessed it by his demeanor. A regular guy,
you ask? Yes. Completely.

He would often corner me and discuss which comedy
sketches he'd liked best on our show the previous week. He was
crazy about the Tim-and-Harvey sketches. He asked me, and yes,
I told him that those guys are as funny in real life as they are on
television.

"Do you think they'd like to join Barbara and me one Saturday? With their wives, of course."

I said I was sure they would. I gave him Tim's home number, being pretty sure he wouldn't mind getting a phone call from Cary Grant.

I called Tim to give him a heads-up nonetheless.

"Hello?"

"Hey, Tim. It's Carol. You're going to be getting a call from Cary Grant."

"Who?"

"Cary Grant, yep."

I explained. We hung up. Cary Grant called him on Wednesday and issued an invitation to Tim and his wife, Sharkey, and then Harvey and his wife, Debby, to join them at the track on Saturday. Within a nanosecond Sharkey and Debby were off and running to the Galleria in search of the perfect outfits for a Saturday afternoon at the track with Cary Grant.

The afternoon went swimmingly. Cary was charming (surprise) and quite possibly the best audience Conway and Korman had ever had. He was smitten with the two of them, who happened to be on a roll that day. And why not? They had Cary Grant in stitches.

The Kormans and the Conways drove home on cloud nine. What a day!

Cary called Tim the following Wednesday. Bam! Off to the Galleria again.

Once again, Saturday at the racetrack, and once again the boys were really on. They reported back that there were times when Cary could hardly catch his breath, he was laughing so hard.

Driving home, Harvey and Tim were a little concerned at this point. "How can we keep this up? I think we've used up all of our shtick!"

Wednesday came around again, and with it another invitation to the Grants' private box.

As far as Cary was concerned, all Tim had to say was "Pass the salt," and he would be put away. But as far as the boys went, this third Saturday was work. They just didn't want to let Cary down. Of course they didn't. The following week, they tried to think up other bits that would floor him, unable to bear the possibility that they might disappoint him. While Cary was still happy as a clam, after the next couple of Saturdays, Harvey and Tim were bordering on nervous exhaustion.

Now here comes one of my favorite lines in this whole world.

At the usual time on Wednesday, the phone rang at the Conways' residence.

TIM: If that's Cary Grant, I'm not home.

Adrienne Lenore Weingardt

*

Harvey and I were rehearsing a very funny sketch called "The Pail." He was a psychiatrist and I was a first-time patient. My problem was that I couldn't get over the childhood trauma of the school bully who stole my pail out of the sandbox when we were seven years old. It still haunted me, and I was hoping this famous doctor could curb my ongoing anxiety. The upshot of the sketch is that the psychiatrist himself turns out to be the school bully, who for years has hoarded sand pails in a closet in his office.

As his patient, I demand that he give me back my pail. He reluctantly hands me a pail, and just as I'm about to leave, I look at it closely and say, "Wait a minute! This isn't *my* pail! My pail had Minnie Mouse painted on it. This one has Donald Duck! This pail belongs to Barbara Brown! GIVE ME *MY* PAIL!" The sketch ends with Harvey relinquishing my original pail and even having to reach into his inner jacket pocket to hand me the matching spade.

I didn't think the name Barbara Brown was terribly interesting, so when we rehearsed it again I came out with, "This pail belonged to Adrienne Lenore Weingardt!"

"Where'd that name come from?" I was asked.

"It's the name of a girl I was in grammar school with. I haven't seen her since. I think there were only eleven or twelve of us, and when we graduated from the sixth grade, we went to different junior high schools."

But the name stuck with me, I guess, because here it was coming out of me after all this time.

The show aired a week later, and on Monday morning, the phone rang in my office and Rae Whitney, my assistant, took the call. It was a woman calling from Nevada.

RAE: May I help you?

WOMAN: Yes. I was watching the Burnett show Saturday night and I heard my name mentioned.

RAE: Oh . . . you must be Miss Weingardt!

WOMAN: That was my maiden name, yes.

RAE: Did you attend the Selma Avenue grammar school in Hollywood?

WOMAN: Yes . . .

RAE: Well, you and Carol were in the same class.

Pause.

WOMAN: I don't remember her.

Carol Channing and
Food for Thought

*

I always looked forward to having Carol Channing as a guest on our show. She made every straight line funny, and every funny line funnier. She also had a reputation for never missing a show when she worked on Broadway (2,844 performances in *Hello, Dolly!* alone). She never, ever got sick. She said she owed her remarkable health to what she ate.

Joe and I took Carol out to dinner at Chasen's one night after one of her appearances on our show, and she ordered a plate with nothing on it to be delivered to the table. That done, she reached down into a picnic cooler she had brought with her, unwrapped a slab of raw blubber, and slapped it down on the plate. I figured she must know *something*, because it sure worked for her. However, I wasn't about to give it a whirl myself.

We booked Carol for another guest appearance the following season. That Monday morning before the reading with the cast and writers, we got a call from Carol's husband saying she was under the weather and couldn't make it in that day, but not

Carol Channing and me on The Carol Burnett Show.

to worry, she'd definitely be fine come Tuesday. I wondered what was wrong.

Carol was there as promised the next morning, bright-eyed as could be. I asked her how she felt.

"Ohhh! Darlin', I'm FINE now, just fine!" Her smile, as usual, was a mile wide.

"What happened?"

"Well, we were playing Vegas last week, and I had this frozen elk flown in."

"Frozen elk?"

"YES! And it just hit me the wrong way. Boy, did I learn a lesson!"

She leaned in close to me and took my hand. Those huge eyes were glued to my face and staring at me very seriously. We were nose to nose. She said in that low voice of hers, "Carol, you MUST listen to me, and don't ever forget this."

I nodded.

"Whenever you're on the road, you must NEVER eat just any old elk."

I've managed to keep that promise to this day.

Lucy

❋

I first met Lucille Ball nearly a decade before *The Carol Burnett Show* got its start. In fact, I met her when she came to see me in *Once upon a Mattress*. Opening night was May 11, 1959, at an off-Broadway theater, the Phoenix. This was my big break. At last, here I was, playing the lead in a George Abbott musical. The overture began, and I felt as if my chest was about to blow wide open with every note played. I'm not sure how I got through the show without passing out from stage fright, but I did.

The next day, the reviews were positive, and we were off and running!

That evening we were all buzzing around backstage, thrilled over our opening night response and getting ready for our second performance, when someone shouted, "Lucy's out front!"

I peeked through the curtain and spotted this shock of orange hair in the middle of the second row. *Omigod. Lucy.* I never should have looked. If I had thought I was scared to death the night before. . . .

Somehow I remembered everything I was supposed to do, and the next thing I knew, we were taking our bows. Lucy was out there on her feet, clapping away.

A few minutes later there was a knock on my dressing room door. I opened it and there she stood.

"Kid, you were terrific." She walked into the tiny room and aimed for the couch, which had a nasty-looking spring sticking out of it. I was about to warn her when she said, "Don't worry. I see it." She sat down on the other end.

She stayed about thirty minutes, making me feel like a prom queen, and as she got up to leave, she said, "Kid, if you ever need me for anything, just give me a call. Promise?" I nodded. She gave me a hug and left.

A few years later, still well before *The Carol Burnett Show*, CBS said they'd air a Carol Burnett special if I could come up with a major guest star. Bob Banner, who would be producing the special, said, "Well, maybe you should call Lucy."

I knew Lucy was busy with her show, and I hesitated to call her because I was scared she'd think I was being pushy.

Banner and CBS kept encouraging me to call her. So finally I did.

"Hey, kid, what's up?" Couldn't mistake that voice.

Embarrassed, I mumbled something about a CBS special, and that they "wanted me to have . . . and I know how busy you are . . . so please don't think . . ."

But I never got out the next few words.

"When do you need me?"

I told her, and she was there.

Lucy and me singing "Chutzpah" from
Carol + 2, *January 1967.*

Lucy, Zero, and
Carol + 2

*

The show was called *Carol + 2*. It was written by the wonderful comedy writer Nat Hiken, and it featured a great musical number for Lucy and me called "Chutzpah" (which brought the TV studio audience to their feet), written by Ken and Mitzie Welch. The other guest was the phenomenal Zero Mostel. He sang "If I Were a Rich Man," from his great hit show, *Fiddler on the Roof.* Even in a tuxedo he was totally convincing as his character, Tevye.

So we did it. No dancers, no singers, just the three of us. Simple, clean, and funny. No hassles, no problems. Except for one thing: it was sponsored by American Motors.

Okay, let me try to explain this.

Nat had written a wonderfully funny sketch for Zero and me called "Tenth Anniversary," in which we were such lowlifes that we made *The Honeymooners* look like the Kennedys. Zero and I play a couple that has been married for ten years; today is their anniversary, and they can't stand the sight of each other. They are both slobs, living in a dump, and arguing all the time. In the middle of one of their blowups the phone rings and they learn that the judge who had performed their marriage ceremony ten years ago wasn't a real judge, soooo . . . they aren't legally married! The twist, of course, is that all of a sudden they become sexually attracted to each other—forbidden fruit and all that.

From there on, the sketch gets wilder and wilder, with Zero's character chasing my character all over the room, trying to seduce her. She, naturally, loves every moment of it, flirting like crazy and acting as coquettishly as possible. My character's name in the sketch was Florence.

I only wish I could put on this page what Zero Mostel did with that name. When his character started to get the hots for Florence, he turned that ordinary name into a three-act play. The sounds he made were astonishing. His voice took the elevator down into his very bowels. "FLO-RENCE! FL-OO-REEN-CE! F-L-O-R-E-N-C-E!" He sounded like a rhinoceros in heat. The dress rehearsal audience went crazy.

After the dress rehearsal ended, all of us were basking in the audience response. I was in my dressing room getting ready for the air show, with its new audience including the sponsors and their wives, when our associate producer, Bob Wright, knocked on the door and came in with a representative from American Motors. I don't remember his name. Let's call him Warren.

WARREN: Miss Burnett, the show is wonderful. American Motors is very proud to be sponsoring it.
ME: Thank you so much!
WARREN: Ah . . . however, we have to request a slight change in the script before the next show.
ME: Yes?
WARREN: In that skit you do with Mr. Mostel . . .
ME: Yes? *(I'm thinking they might feel we were going a*

> *little overboard in the horny department, when we*
> *learn we're not married, and would like us to tone*
> *it down.)*

WARREN: I'm afraid you can't use the name Florence.

ME: Excuse me?

WARREN: You see, the head of American Motors, our boss . . . well, that's his wife's name.

ME: Yes?

WARREN: Well, in the context of your little skit, it could be taken as offensive. Please use another name.

ME: But Mr. Mostel has been using that name in our rehearsals for two whole weeks. He has made the audience scream with laughter simply by the *way* he says it. I can't ask him to, *what,* call me Gloria? At this late hour? It could throw him completely! I can't do that to him!

WARREN: I'm sorry, but that's our decision. Above all we don't want to upset our boss and his wife when they see the show tonight.

That said, he opened the door and left.

I think I threw a powder puff across the room. Bob and I just stood there staring at each other. The stupidity of it all was mind-boggling. I said something lame like, "You think Florence, Italy, would sue?"

Then I got an idea. . . .

"Bob, let's find Warren's boss. I want to talk to him."

Bob looked a little nervous. "Are you sure about this?"

"This is between us. Don't tell anybody else. Let's just find him before the show!"

We located Warren's boss and had him call the dressing room. I thanked him for returning my call so quickly and launched into my pitch. "I know you and your wife are coming

Zero Mostel coming on to Florence in Carol + 2.

COURTESY OF CAROL BURNETT

to the show tonight, and I have to let you in on a little secret! Zero Mostel and I are doing a very funny scene, and I thought it would be fun to surprise your wife by using her name for my character!"

He all but did a tap dance over the phone. I made him

promise not to tell his wife. Gleefully he promised, thanked me, and hung up after saying, "Florence will be delighted! What a wonderful surprise!"

After the show, he and his wife came backstage, and she was *beaming* as she told us she couldn't wait to tell all her friends about our using her name in the sketch. I looked around and spotted Warren. He was grinning from ear to ear, nodding like crazy, and looking pleased as punch. I looked over at him and grinned right back.

A word about Nat Hiken, who wrote that show. He was the comedy genius behind *The Phil Silvers Show.* When Nat came on board for *Carol + 2,* he wrote everything for the entire show with the exception of the musical number "Chutzpah," by the Welches. He conceived and wrote every one of the sketches we did, and they were some of the funniest pieces of material I have ever had the joy of performing. I think *Carol + 2* had the smallest staff of any major TV special ever created, before or since. It was unheard of then, and would certainly be unheard of these days. And it turned out swell. Sad to say, Nat died shortly after we did the show. He was a lovely and very funny man.

And as for Lucy, well . . . that special was amazing fun, and it wouldn't have happened without her.

This happened in January 1967.

That fall, our show premiered on CBS.

Dinner with Lucy at the Farmers' Market

*

After the special, Lucy and I were in touch often, and I was thrilled when she asked me to be a guest on *Here's Lucy* and *The Lucy Show*, which came after *I Love Lucy*. Lucille Ball had a reputation for being tough. There were times on the set when she'd say things to someone on the crew or to the writers that could've been considered blunt, to say the least, but she was always *right*. She never censored her opinions or couched them euphemistically. She called it the way she saw it. If she didn't like something, she let you know. And if she *did* like something, she was as complimentary as could be. That's why the crew and staff loved her. She was honest—and none of the criticism was ever personal.

In those days, though, it was unheard of for a woman to run a show, let alone to run it "like a man." All of the greats—Caesar, Berle, Gleason, et cetera—could say whatever they very well pleased, and their reputations remained intact. They were tough, and that was to be expected, but a woman being tough? There was a name for that, and it wasn't complimentary.

One of my favorite pictures with Lucy.
COURTESY OF CAROL BURNETT

* * *

Once I had my own variety show, Lucy and I would do trade-offs. I'd go on one of her shows, and she would guest-star on one of mine. We became close friends. She always sent me flowers on my birthday, and I would always save the card.

One week when she was on our show, we went across the street to a Chinese restaurant in the Farmers' Market, before the evening orchestra rehearsal. The two of us slid into a booth, and as we were perusing the menu, she looked at me and said, "Kid, you're so lucky to have Joe producing your show, running interference, being the bad cop."

I agreed with her. It wasn't in my nature to be the boss. I was a first-class chicken. When I didn't care for a comedy sketch, I couldn't come right out and say it wasn't working. No, I would say to the writers, "Gosh, guys, it's not your fault, I'm just not doing this *right*. Can you help me? Maybe come up with a different line or two? I'm really *sorry*." Joe would simply say, "This isn't working. It's not funny. Fix it." I could never do that. Those words would stick in my throat. So, yes, Lucy was correct in her assessment of how our show was being run.

"Y'know," she continued, "when I was married to the Cuban, I never had to worry about a thing. Desi was so damn smart about *everything*—scripts, cameras, lighting, costuming, you name it. I would simply waltz in on Monday mornings and the cast and I would read a perfect script, all ready for rehearsal. All *I* had to do was be Lucy. Desi took care of the rest. We made a great team. Plus it didn't hurt that we were crazy about each other . . . just like you and Joe. Unfortunately, we split up. But it was great while it lasted."

We ordered and then were quiet for a while. She lit up a cigarette. Then she chuckled.

"Y'know, after Desi and I parted, it was all on my shoulders. *I Love Lucy* was over. Now I was Lucy in a different format for CBS. I had a great sidekick in Gale Gordon. I had a great time slot. So far so good. All I needed was a great show."

She got quiet again. The egg rolls arrived.

By this time, I wasn't that hungry; I was waiting for the next installment of Lucy's story. She put out her cigarette and took a bite of an egg roll. We chewed for a bit, and then she continued.

"I remember the Monday morning when I went to the studio for our first rehearsal, and TA-DA! Guess what? The script stank. I mean, it STANK! I was thrown but good. I needed to catch my breath, so I suggested that we all take a break and come back after lunch. I sat in my office, trying to figure out what to do, how to handle the situation. Could the Lucy I had always been be able to actually run a show? Would anybody listen to her? I knew I had to turn into Desi, be fearless, or there'd be no show."

She paused, then went on. "I got back to the writers' room after lunch and sat in the big black leather chair at the head of the conference table. Everyone was quiet. You coulda heard a pin drop. I opened up and told them what I thought about the script in no uncertain terms, no pussyfooting around. They got the picture and went back to work in a hurry."

She lit another cigarette and smiled. "And *that*, kid, is when they added the *S* to the end of my last name."

I laughed right through the kumquats.

I miss her. She died early on the morning of my birthday in 1989, and I got my flowers and the card from her that afternoon.

Jody and Ray Charles

*

Joe and I had three daughters, Carrie, Jody, and Erin. They were all pretty close in age, and pretty much a happy handful.

Sometime in 1971 we were all at home, watching *The Ed Sullivan Show* on television. Joe, our three little girls, and I were all piled together on the bed in our room. Ray Charles was introduced on the show and began singing. Jody, who was about four years old at the time, crawled down off the bed, walked over to the TV set, put her little hands on the screen, and kissed Ray Charles's face. She just stood there and whispered "I love you" to his image.

Not long after that incident, I walked in on a conversation she was having with a plumber who was working on our kitchen sink, and I heard her say, "Ray Charles is my husband, you know."

The plumber smiled. "No kiddin'?"

"Oh yes."

"How long you two been married?"

"Twenty years. He can't see anything, you know, so I have to lead him everywhere."

A couple of years later, Ray was a guest on our show. I told him that Jody, now about six, was probably his biggest fan (along with being his youngest wife). He laughed and asked if she ever came to the taping. I assured him, "Oh, she'll be here. She wouldn't miss seeing you for the world."

After the show, a few of us were in my dressing room along with the kids. There was a knock on the door, and Ray walked in with his manager. Jody's eyes turned into Ping-Pong balls.

Ray stretched out his arms. "Is my little Jody here?"

I took her hand and led her over to him. "Ray, this is Jody."

She was looking up at him adoringly, and he reached down, picked her up, held her in his arms, and gave her a big kiss on the cheek. Tears rolled down her face as she wrapped her arms around his neck. Ray had a tear or two as well.

In fact, I don't think there was a dry eye in the room.

LEFT TO RIGHT: *Carrie, Joe, Jody, me,*
and baby Erin, 1968.

Erin and Diplomacy

*

When you have three young daughters close in age, between four and seven in our case, it's always an adventure taking them out to a restaurant. We liked living dangerously, so we tried it fairly often. Usually one of the girls would be good and the other two difficult at best: "I don't want any vegetables!" "She took my butter!" "This is *my* napkin!" "Mom, Jody's kicking me under the table!" Sometimes we'd get lucky and *two* would behave in a somewhat civilized manner, leaving Joe and me to deal with whichever one was destined to be the evening's handful.

Our restaurant of choice was a neighborhood Italian family restaurant that catered to kids and early diners. Feeling brave one evening, we piled the girls in the car and headed for calamari-and-cannoli land. We were led to our booth, where seating arrangements were as follows: Carrie, me, Erin, Joe, Jody. Joe and I always put Erin between us because she was the baby. I'm not sure of the logic in that, but that's what we always did. Menus came and went. Carrie and Jody were actually ordering meals we approved of, and didn't seem to be itching for a bread fight. So far so good. That left Erin. The waiter took her menu and asked Miss Four-year-old what she'd like for dinner.

"Nothing, thanks. I'll just have dessert." I looked down at her and said what we all expect ourselves as parents to say under these circumstances: "Excuse me, missy, but no dinner, no dessert." She folded her arms across her chest, stuck out her chin, and said, "Fine."

Carrie and Jody were in hog heaven, scarfing down their salads, their veggies, and whatever else was green, thrilled that Erin was in deep doo-doo.

Time ticked by.

Erin, arms crossed defiantly, kept sneaking looks at me. If I looked back at her, she'd quickly turn her head away, not wanting to make eye contact. Dinner dragged on. She'd look at me, I'd look at her, and she'd look away. I knew Erin wanted to make up, but she wasn't willing to make the first move. I just figured I'd let her dangle there and then we'd head for home.

Dinner was almost over and we were about to ask for the check when Erin looked up at her father and said, "I love you, Daddy."

"I love you, too, Erin."

"And I also love your wife."

I laughed so hard I let her have dessert.

My Chum Julie Andrews

*

The year was 1961. I was still doubling on *The Garry Moore Show* and *Once upon a Mattress*. Julie Andrews was already a full-fledged Broadway star thanks to her performance in *My Fair Lady*. Now she was playing Queen Guinevere opposite Richard Burton in *Camelot*.

We first met when Julie came to see me in *Mattress*. The night she attended, she was accompanied by her manager, Lew Wilson, and Bob Banner, the producer of *The Garry Moore Show*. Both men had touted us (separately) to each other, saying, "You two girls will hit it off like crazy! You simply *have* to meet."

Later, long after that evening, after we *had* hit it off like crazy, we both laughed at the fact that when someone pushes you like that, the natural impulse is to run the other way—an impulse we both felt at that first meeting backstage after the curtain. That first night we had arranged to go to a Chinese restaurant after the show. I shoved my Yorkshire terrier, Bruce, into my tote bag and off we went to Ruby Foo's.

Lew and Bob sat across from us. Bruce, in her tote bag, was

on the floor between us, every once in a while sticking her nose up and out to sniff at the chop suey. It took Julie and me a good five minutes of sizing each other up before the dam burst. Then we started talking, telling stories, laughing like crazy, and not letting the men get a word in edgewise. As I remember, we wound up closing the place.

That was the beginning.

Bob booked Julie as a guest on *The Garry Moore Show.* Ken Welch, who had been my coach and special material writer for about four years, was a fill-in that week for our musical writer, Ed Scott, who was ailing. I had suggested Ken to Garry, who welcomed him on board. Ken came up with a fabulous finale for Julie and me based on the Broadway show tune "Big D" from *The Most Happy Fella.* We performed it in cowboy outfits with ten-gallon hats, oversized fuzzy chaps, and boots.

The number began and off we went! It felt like the two of us had been separated at birth and were rediscovering each other on the playground, having a ball. I'm not sure, but I think it was one of the first times ever that the audience for a weekly television show gave a finale a standing ovation. The place went nuts. Julie and I were thrilled to bits about the reception, and dear Garry was beaming. It felt like an opening night on Broadway.

That night the idea was born that Julie and I should do a television special together, and that Ken Welch would be one of the creators. Bob Banner took the brainstorm to CBS, with the title *Julie and Carol at Carnegie Hall.*

CBS didn't exactly do cartwheels.

Quote: "Nobody knows Julie Andrews west of New Jersey." (She hadn't yet done a movie at this point in time.) "And we see Carol on Garry's show every week. In other words, what's so special about this special?"

OVERLEAF: *Rehearsing for the Carnegie Hall special with Julie.*
COURTESY OF CAROL BURNETT

Over the next few weeks, Bob Banner, Joe, Lew Wilson, and other representatives of ours did their best to convince CBS that they should buy the show. No dice.

It was a rainy afternoon in New York during the week between Christmas and New Year's. I was attending an affiliates' luncheon at CBS, sitting at Garry Moore's table, along with Mike Dann and Oscar Katz (two of the network's major players). I was in the mood to kid them about turning up their noses at Julie and me. "Y'know, maybe my chum and I should go over to NBC. At least *they* have color!" (CBS hadn't made the leap yet.) They chuckled and changed the subject. I politely kept nudging them, and they politely smiled, ignoring me while polishing off their Bloody Marys.

When lunch was over, we all rode down in the elevator together. Outside on Madison Avenue, it was raining like crazy, and Oscar offered to help me hail a cab. None was to be found. He offered to wait with me until I got one. Thanking him, I said, "Oh, don't worry. You go on. Somebody in a truck will pull up and I'll hitch a ride."

I'd barely gotten out those words when a huge beer truck stopped in front of us at the curb and the burly, tattooed driver leaned across the seat and yelled out the passenger window, "Hey, Carol! Me and the missus watch ya all the time on *Garry*! Need a lift?"

Oscar Katz and Mike Dann hoisted me into the cab of the truck, and as it pulled away I leaned out the window to wish them a happy New Year. Their mouths were still hanging open as they waved me on my way.

The driver deposited me in front of my building, and as I ran down the hall to my apartment I could hear the phone ringing. It stopped just as I put the key in the lock. Before I could get my coat off, it started to ring again.

"Hello, Carol. Oscar Katz. Okay, you got your show."

Julie and me on our last special, Together Again.

"What? Really?"

"That was pretty peculiar, what happened. We figure it's an omen of some kind. Anyhow, congratulations."

And that's how *Julie and Carol at Carnegie Hall* got sold.

Ken Welch and Mike Nichols came on board and wrote the

whole show. The night of the taping, New York experienced a huge snowstorm; I had always felt rain and snow were signs of good luck, so this storm was right on schedule. The show aired in March 1962 and won super ratings and lots of prizes. It was the first American television show to win the coveted Golden Rose of Montreux. I'm just sorry I never got that truck driver's name.

Through the years that followed, Julie and I kept in touch. She went to Hollywood, and everybody west of New Jersey got to know her and helped make her one of the most popular movie stars of all time, winning the Oscar for *Mary Poppins* for starters.

I stayed with television. Even though I did a few movies, I preferred (and was better at) weekly comedy-variety and playing to a live audience, thanks to the super training I got from Garry Moore. However, Julie and I did get together for two more TV specials, *Julie and Carol at Lincoln Center* in 1971 and *Julie and Carol Together Again* in 1989.

We joke that during the first show all we talked about was our careers and our love lives. The second time around all we talked about was our kids and our husbands. The third time we were very much into the subject of menopause.

If we ever do another one, we've decided to call it *A Metamucil Musical with Julie and Carol.*

A Very Bad Hair Day

*

Julie Andrews and I were working on our second TV special in New York for CBS, this one at Lincoln Center. Joe was producing and the Welches were writing the special material and music. Ernie Flatt was the choreographer, Dave Powers was directing, and Peter Matz was the musical director—all of them creators from our variety show. It was 1971, nine years after Julie and I had done our first show at Carnegie Hall. Julie was a major movie star now, and I had had my own weekly TV show for four years. We were very excited to be back together again. Even though we had husbands and kids now, we both reverted right back to the time we first met—giggling like schoolgirls, acting up, making jokes, and generally having one helluva grand ol' time.

The show was to air in December, but we were taping it in the summertime. I remember telling everybody to be on the lookout for a rainstorm on taping day, given my feeling that rain was good luck. After our final dress rehearsal, Joe and I went

165

back to the hotel to order room service and turn in early before the big day.

That night I was having a rough time getting to sleep, so I got up around midnight to get a drink of water. I looked into the bathroom mirror and had a brilliant idea: I should highlight my hair! I figured a blond streak here and there would give my hair more oomph for the show the next day.

There was an all-night drugstore on the same block as our hotel, so I dressed quietly so as not to wake Joe, and tiptoed out of the room. A few minutes later I was back with a bottle of peroxide. Joe was still asleep. I put on a robe and locked myself in the bathroom. Parting my hair in sections, I began to comb the peroxide into random strands all over my head. How difficult could highlighting be?

What was I thinking, you ask? The answer: I wasn't.

Expecting to see immediate results, I kept combing and combing until the bottle was empty. Still no results. I figured I'd bought a faulty bottle, so I towel-dried my hair and went to bed.

The next morning I awoke to shouts of "OMIGOD! What happened to you?" Joe was beside himself. I ran into the bathroom and looked into the mirror. I started to cry as I explained what I'd done the night before to create this fright wig, which was now the color and texture of *straw*. I looked like Ray Bolger in *The Wizard of Oz*. No, I looked like I had returned from the grave. Joe just stood there shaking his head in disbelief.

We got to Lincoln Center for our morning rehearsal before the audience was due in. After I removed my baseball cap, our hairdresser, Ernie Adler, took one look at me and literally clutched at his chest, breathing heavily. "What in the hell did you do to yourself?"

"Ernie! Can't you do something to fix this awful mess?"

Julie and Carol at Lincoln Center: *my bad hair day.*

Showtime was only a couple of hours away. Ernie did his best by washing my hair and using tons of conditioner to give it a little life. It was an improvement, but it wasn't nearly enough.

To this day, every time I see a picture of Julie and me in that special, I cringe. But the show must go on, and on it went. Julie and I did the opening number, and the audience was enthusiastic and ready to have fun. I tried to forget my hair and what the audience might be thinking about it: *Did a small blond animal die on her head?*

Later in the show there was a comedic musical segment where I played the world's oldest living ballerina on yet another final farewell tour, reprising her most famous role as a Greek goddess. Bob Mackie outfitted me in a tacky white wig (which, actually, was a notch better than my own hair), a pouchy stomach, and boobs down to my waist. The theme of the ballet was Greek gods and goddesses. Julie Andrews was playing my young and gorgeous rival for the affections of a beautiful hunk of a god (our lead dancer, Don Crichton). The plot has me preparing to seduce this young god, but before I can make much progress my gorgeous rival bowls him over with a very sexy dance. He succumbs to her charms, and in a fit of rage my character brings down a curse on her rival:

O mighty Thor! Creator of lightning and storm! Ruler of the heavens and most powerful of all the gods! I beseech you! Strike down this beautiful stranger . . . NOW!

I *swear* that on the very tail end of that bit of dialogue there was a genuine, honest-to-God clap of thunder that rattled the theater windows, and it began to pour outside. I got my rain. The timing was perfect. And I felt wonderful!

So in spite of the trauma of the tresses, I wound up having yet another rollicking and utterly magical good time with my chum. This second TV special was also well received. And believe it or not, after it aired I got several letters from viewers wanting to know where I got my hair done!

Julie, Mike Nichols, and the Lady in the Elevator

*

Julie Andrews is a very funny and very bawdy lady. She's a true dame in both the British sense and in the other (good) sense of the word—she's down-to-earth, laughs loud and hard, and loves to play practical jokes.

We were together again in Washington, D.C., in January 1964 to take part in a show to honor President Lyndon Johnson. Celebrities were pouring in from Hollywood and New York to perform. Julie and I were going to sing the medley of Broadway musicals that we had done at Carnegie Hall. Joe and I had arrived the night before the show, around ten o'clock, and checked into the hotel where everybody connected with the gala was staying. I called Julie's room, figuring she and her husband, Tony Walton, had also just arrived.

"Hey chum, we're here. Just got in. We're unpacking," I told her.

"Great! What room are you in?"

Our rooms turned out to be on the same floor.

She said that she and Tony were already in their PJs and

170

robes and had ordered some hot chocolate. "Why don't you put on your robes and fuzzy slippers and come down to our room?" Joe was reluctant to walk down the hall in fuzzy slippers and a robe, but I was gung-ho, so he threw on a sweatsuit and I put on my flannels, and off we went to Julie and Tony's suite.

We were all on our second cup of hot chocolate when the phone rang and Julie picked up. "Ohhh, Mike! You're here! Great. What floor are you on? . . . Well, we're down on the second floor having hot chocolate with Carol and Joe. C'mon down!"

It was Mike Nichols calling from his room on the fourth floor. He said he'd be down after he hung up a few things. Mike and Elaine May were also going to be in the show, doing one of their classic comedy bits.

A few minutes later Julie's face lit up.

"What?"

She looked at me and said, "Let's go down the hall and greet Mike in our jammies when he comes out of the elevator. There's a settee right in front of the elevator and we can sit there and wait for him. He'll get a big kick out of seeing us dressed like this!"

I had to admit we looked somewhat ridiculous (I think it was the big fuzzy slippers), so I figured, why not?

We left Tony and Joe and went down the hall, plopped ourselves on the settee, and watched the numbers above the elevator light up as it ascended and descended. We figured that when the number 4 stayed lit up for a moment, it would be Mike getting into the elevator on his way down. So far, no action.

Julie got that look again. "When the door opens and Mike comes out, let's be *kissing!*"

"WHAT?"

"I don't mean actually *kissing* kissing. Let's just *pretend* to be kissing! He'll absolutely *scream!*"

We figured out a way to hug and make our faces disappear

171

in each other's necks so that it would look like we were in a mad liplock.

We kept staring at the numbers, and finally the number 4 lit up for a few seconds. The elevator went *ding-ding* as the car approached our floor.

Julie and I grabbed each other and began our charade. We heard the elevator door open. We heard someone walk out and then we heard the door close. We didn't hear anything else.

It was very quiet. Too quiet. I whispered to Julie, "I'm not sure it's Mike. What do you think? I mean, he would've said *something*." Julie whispered back, "Well, we can't stay like this forever." We broke our clinch and looked up.

A woman who was the spitting image of Lady Bird Johnson was making her way down the hall with a couple of burly men who looked a lot like Secret Service, all of them looking back at us over their shoulders. Julie and I were frozen with embarrassment. They disappeared around the corner. *Oh God, was that really the First Lady?* Before we could get up to run back to Julie's room, the woman returned to peek around the corner . . . and looked straight at *me*!

"Aren't you Carol Burnett?" she asked sweetly, in an unmistakable Texas accent.

Pointing to my chum, who was looking up at the ceiling as innocent as a newborn, I replied, "Yes, ma'am, and this here is Mary Poppins!"

Laurence Olivier

*

During the 1970s when our show was on the air, Joe and I bought a small beach house in Malibu, where we spent weekends and summers with the kids. The real estate lady who sold it to us was constantly pressing us to rent the house if for some reason we weren't planning on using it for any length of time. We would always say no. I didn't want to have strangers in our home, and I *really* didn't want to be somebody's landlord.

One Friday in 1975, I got a call in my dressing room just as we were getting ready to tape the show. I picked up the phone. It was Pat, the real estate lady. I rolled my eyes at Joe and mouthed her name to him.

She sounded absolutely giddy. "Carol, I have someone who wants to rent the beach house for the whole summer! I quoted a big fat price and they said fine!"

Joe took the phone from me and for the hundredth time repeated our mantra about not renting. I motioned to Joe to give

173

me back the phone. I thought I'd have a little fun with Pat before we hung up.

"Pat, how about this? No more calls about renting the house unless it's Laurence Olivier! Okay?"

Pat paused. Then she said, "Well, I guess you're gonna be a landlord, then."

"What?"

"Guess who wants to rent your house."

I almost fell out of my chair.

Laurence Olivier. He was filming *Marathon Man* that summer, and our house was perfect for him and his family.

He turned out to be a swell tenant.

One Saturday night he and his wife, Joan Plowright, threw a party. It felt funny being invited to our own house for dinner, but everybody had a fine time. I remember asking him what his favorite film role was. He replied, "Well, I can tell you one thing, it wasn't Heathcliff in *Wuthering Heights.*"

We all protested: "You've got to be kidding! You were wonderful! So strong and romantic," et cetera, et cetera.

He said, "I can re-create my performance for you here and now," whereupon he walked over to the large fireplace in the dining room, turned his back to us, and leaned his hands against the mantel, letting his head drop in an oh-so-melancholy way.

You could've heard a pin drop.

Finally, in a whisper, he said, "Cathy," the name of his sweetheart, whom Merle Oberon played in the movie. "Cathy . . ." I had never swooned before, but I felt my knees start to buckle.

He said "Cathy" one more time, then turned back to us. "That's about it. My performance in a nutshell. Bugs Bunny could've done it."

I totally disagreed with his assessment, and based on the expressions on the other women's faces, I was not alone.

Walter Matthau

*

I t was 1972 and *The Carol Burnett Show* was in the middle of its run. There was never a day at work that wasn't fun. The way we worked was also extremely efficient. I once totaled up my weekly hours spent rehearsing and taping the show, and it came to about thirty. I had a *part-time job*! We were probably one of the most organized television shows ever. Anyhow, that was our reputation. We produced a mini Broadway musical revue every week and still had time to go home for an early dinner every night with the kids, except for Friday, when we taped the show.

I suspect this was because most of the cast, writers, and crew came from theater and live TV. Also, Joe was a terrific producer. Boy, did he know how to run a tight ship. He had begun his training as a writer on the wonderful *Dinah Shore Show* and graduated to producer under the expert tutelage of executive producer Bob Banner on *The Garry Moore Show*. When Gloria Swanson appeared as a guest on my show, she was absolutely stunned at how fast we worked and learned.

Starting on Monday we learned our lines, our music, and our dances, hit our marks, and rehearsed. Come Friday, we taped the show twice in front of two different audiences, one at five o'clock and one at eight o'clock, and were finished early enough to have a nice, quiet dinner at Chasen's. On Saturdays Joe would edit the show, choosing the best takes from both performances, finishing in time for a round of golf. No hassle. Hardly ever a retake.

It was a dream job. We had weekends, summers, and Christmas and Easter off, plus a few weeks here and there in between. It was a school schedule, which suited our family to a T. Did I mention the fun part? Not a day went by when there wasn't a huge belly laugh (or several) ringing through the rehearsal halls of CBS Television City. We were blessed, all right. Television was my second home. And the people who created our show were my second family.

I had acted in one movie, *Who's Been Sleeping in My Bed?* in 1963, with Dean Martin and Elizabeth Montgomery—one of those sixties comedies that was about as substantial as cotton candy. I'm not knocking it: sometimes cotton candy can be satisfying when that's what you're in the mood for. There just wasn't much to it, that's all. I played the best friend of the leading lady, sort of the Eve Arden role. While I had a good time with everybody, I wasn't crazy about the medium: lots of sitting around and waiting. So it never bothered me that the movie studios weren't ringing my doorbell. I was a warhorse. I liked rehearsing. And when the curtain went up I liked performing in front of an audience and then going home. Besides, I wasn't the movie star type.

So it came as a bit of a surprise one night when our doorbell rang and there stood Walter Matthau.

I'm getting ahead of myself here.

The previous week my agent had received a call about the

possibility of my being in a movie called *Pete 'n' Tillie* with Walter Matthau. The script was sent over, and I read it and loved it. Not only would I be co-starring with one of the biggest stars in the movies, but it was also going to be directed by Martin Ritt *(Hud)* and written by Julius Epstein *(Casablanca)*.

Why me? At that time, television performers were television performers and movie stars were movie stars. The crossover thing hadn't much happened yet, with the exception of James Garner and Steve McQueen. Still, a meeting was set up and Walter Matthau, Martin Ritt, and Julius Epstein were coming over to our house to meet with me and talk.

Joe and I opened the door and there they were. We invited them in. Martin Ritt reminded me of a friendly bear. Julius Epstein was nattily turned out and very witty. Walter Matthau was funny but somewhat intimidating.

I would be Tillie to Walter's Pete. We would be filming during the summer hiatus from our show, which was perfect timing for me. The three men were very enthusiastic, which was contagious.

I said yes immediately. When the meeting was over, there were lots of handshakes and smiles. I stood in the doorway and waved goodbye, grinning from ear to ear, thanking them and saying, "See you soon!"

I closed the door and leaned against it. Joe took one look at my face and said, "What's the matter?"

I was terrified. "Oh Lord. They're big-screen and I'm little-screen!"

The first few days of filming began, and even though I didn't have much to do in those particular scenes, I felt like a stick. Everybody else was loose as a goose. I was in awe watching Geraldine Page, Barry Nelson, and of course Walter being inventive every which way they turned. Even though Martin

Ritt was helpful and friendly, I kept waiting to get my pink slip. Why couldn't I just relax and go with the flow the way I did on my own show? I just couldn't get the feeling that I belonged.

Then Walter asked me to have lunch with him in the commissary. We sat in a booth while I looked over the menu and tried to figure out what to order that would be easy to chew. He made me nervous. *Everything* made me nervous. The conversation was awkward. Walter kept trying to get a complete sentence out of his lunch date, but nothing was happening. Just some nodding and chewing.

Until . . .

WALTER: So tell me, why do you do all this television crap?

ME: *(fork halfway to my mouth)* Excuse me?

WALTER: I said, why do you do all this television crap?

Whoa. Suddenly I found my voice.

ME: Lemme ask you something, Walter. *(This was the first time I had felt comfortable calling him by his first name.)* How many movies do you make a year? Two? Three?

He was one of the most popular actors in the business and was always working, so I knew I was in the ballpark.

WALTER: Yep. That's about right.

ME: Are *all* of them considered great? Or could some fall under the heading of crap?

WALTER: Some of 'em are pretty good, and some of 'em are crap.

Walter and me on the set of Pete 'n' Tillie.

ME: How long do they usually take to film? Ten
           weeks? Twelve weeks?
WALTER: That's about right.
ME: Well, look at it this way, Walter. It takes you
           ten or twelve weeks to make a piece of crap,
           and it takes me just five days.

He threw his head back and laughed. We laughed all the
way through the rest of lunch. In fact, we laughed through the
rest of filming.

Walter, his brilliant and lovely wife, Carol, Joe, and I became fast friends. I was lucky enough to work with him a few more times. Shortly before he died, his son Charley directed us in a television movie, *The Marriage Fool*. On the set one day I reminded Walter about our lunch in the commissary all those years ago. I had always suspected that he had riled me up on purpose.

He looked at me and smiled. "Well, I knew I had to do *something* to loosen you up."

Thank you, Walter.

The Front Page *and*
Mea Culpa

*

"Ladies and gentlemen, please make sure your seat belts are securely fastened; we'll be taking off momentarily."

Joe and I were on a flight to New York for a short visit. The year was 1974. Our show was in its seventh season. The stewardess (that's what they called them then, before "flight attendant" became the proper term) looked at me, smiled, and announced that the movie on our flight was *The Front Page*, starring Jack Lemmon, Walter Matthau, and . . . (indicating me and where I was sitting) Carol Burnett. The other passengers in the cabin turned and smiled at me, and some even waved.

Omigod. No. Please, no. Joe started to laugh.

I had always loved Billy Wilder and his films. When it was announced that he was going to direct Jack and Walter in the classic *The Front Page*, I called his office myself and asked if he'd cast me as the prostitute, Molly Malloy. I also said I'd do it for nothing if they'd donate a sum to charity. I was hired. At one point during the filming, Billy turned to me and said, "You may

Jack Lemmon, me, and Walter in The Front Page, *1974.*
COPYRIGHT © 1978 BILL AVERY/MPTVIMAGES.COM

not be the best actress I've ever directed, but you're definitely the cheapest."

As far as I was concerned, I was also the worst. Here I was, in a movie with the best in the business, and once again I was feeling helpless. I never got a grip on the character, so I acted every scene like I was in a high school play. I yelled every line. No nuance, no subtlety. Let's just say it straight out: no confidence. Even though I had acted in some films by this point, I still harbored that small-screen mentality. What to do? I faced up to the fact that I was going to stink in this picture and couldn't wait until it wrapped.

I purposely didn't see the movie when it opened. I got the reviews I deserved, and happily returned to my own backyard: CBS Television City, for our eighth year. And now here we were on an airplane and they're showing *The Front Page*. It was too late to get off: we had already taxied down the runway and were lifting off.

During the next hour or so, lunch was served. I ate half a roll, dreading the inevitable. It finally arrived. We were asked to lower our window shades, as the movie was about to begin. A few of the passengers smiled at me, and I managed a weak grin back. The cabin darkened and the torture began. I sank as low in my seat as I could and pulled a blanket over me, covering most of my face. When my name first appeared on the screen some folks even clapped. *Where is a parachute when you need one?*

As the movie progressed, I couldn't help peeking at a couple of moments when I was onscreen. Yep, I was as bad as I thought. I returned to my safe haven under the blanket. Mercifully, Joe was asleep.

It was finally over. The window shades were being raised, only this time nobody turned around to smile and wave. Everyone in the entire cabin suddenly seemed very engrossed in the in-flight magazine.

After a while, I climbed over Joe, who must have thought I was heading for the lavatory. Instead, I found the stewardess and made an unusual request: "Do you think I might be able to use your microphone and make an announcement?" She checked with the captain, who said it was okay. (Needless to say, this would never be allowed today.)

She handed me the mike. I tapped it with my finger. It was on.

"Good afternoon, ladies and gentlemen. Hi. This is Carol Burnett. I just happened to be on this flight today and . . . ah . . . I want to take this opportunity to apologize to each and every one of you for my performance in the film you just saw. Thank you."

The entire plane erupted in laughter and applause.

As I climbed back over Joe and into my seat he said, "I don't believe you did that!"

I was grinning from ear to ear, feeling absolutely cleansed.

Restaurant Reservations

✻

In the late 1970s I was in St. Petersburg, Florida, to film *H.E.A.L.T.H.*, a Robert Altman movie. This was my second Altman film. I'd first worked for him in *A Wedding*, and he was my favorite movie director, hands down. He made moviemaking so comfortable. With him I never felt like I didn't belong. And this movie also had a terrific cast headed by James Garner, Lauren Bacall, Glenda Jackson, Paul Dooley, and Dick Cavett.

Becky Mann, my assistant at the time, and I had traveled to Florida a few days ahead of the shooting schedule to get settled in the condos the studio had rented for the cast and crew. We were to film at the famous pink Don CeSar Hotel.

The first night we were there, one of the crew suggested we eat at a local mom-and-pop German restaurant, I think it was called the Happy Times Café. At any rate, it wasn't *that* local, since you had to drive awhile and then go over a toll bridge to get to it. It turned out to be very cozy, and the food was home-cooked and delicious. It was also empty. Mom and Pop were thrilled to see us and pulled out all the stops. We asked them why the restaurant was so empty. They explained that the location was a problem; people didn't want to pay the toll when there were other eateries right in town. We promised to come back as often as we could.

A couple of days later Dick Cavett arrived, and Becky and I took him to the Happy Times. Again, it was delicious, and pretty empty.

After we began shooting I made it a habit to hit the restaurant two or three times a week. Mom and Pop were always thrilled to see us, and made up special dishes for our tasting pleasure.

A few weeks into filming, I decided to ask several of our cast members to be my guests at the good ol' Happy Times for dinner one night, and a great time was had by all. Later that week an article ran in the local paper saying, "Well, the good ol' Happy Times Café was really rocking the other night with the likes of Lauren Bacall, James Garner, Glenda Jackson, Dick Cavett, and Carol Burnett, busy ordering seconds of knockwurst and wiener schnitzel. . . ."

The following Friday I had finished my work for the day, so I asked Becky to call the Happy Times and say we'd be in early.

Mom answered the phone. "Oh dear, I'm so sorry, but we're full."

Is this where the saying "No good deed goes unpunished" comes from?

All My Children

*

I've watched the soap opera *All My Children* (set in the fictional town of Pine Valley) since *before* Erica married the first of her ten husbands. It's the only soap opera I've allowed myself to get hooked on. I used to schedule my lunch hour at work so I could watch it. After VCRs came into being, I would tape the show, just in case I was forced to miss an episode. Sometimes the timer didn't work or the tape would get warped, and I was not a happy camper. I used to talk to our show audience about *All My Children* when I did the introductory Q & A. We even used to do a soap takeoff on our show called *As the Stomach Turns.*

In the early 1980s I was thrilled when the creator of *All My Children*, Agnes Nixon, offered to write a character for me to play as a guest on the show. She came up with a doozy. I was to be the illegitimate child of a carnival con artist and a snake charmer who comes to Pine Valley to find her biological father, who turns out to be Langley Wallingford (the wonderful Louis Edmonds), now married to wealthy socialite Phoebe Tyler (the equally wonderful Ruth Warrick). My name would be Verla Grubbs, and I would look like my name—pure trailer trash. Every outfit was way over the top. My story line was to last for two weeks, or ten episodes. I had several scenes with the late great Eileen Herlie (Myrtle) to boot. I was in heaven.

I flew to New York, where they shot the show, and reported for work, thinking it would be a breeze.

I have never worked so hard in my life. Soaps are not easy! They do a read-through at the crack of dawn. Then there's makeup. Then there's camera blocking. Then there's a run-through with no stops. Then you get into your costume and get ready for the taping. This made for a fourteen-hour workday.

And that was Monday. Now, I also had as many as twenty pages of dialogue to learn for the next day, and the next, and the next. Sometimes just before the countdown the actors would still have scripts in their hands; just seconds before the cameras rolled they'd hide the scripts somewhere—maybe under a pillow on a couch—just in time to say the next line when the camera light went on.

The show was on a tight deadline, so it was taped as if it were live. If you goofed or forgot a line, there was no stopping or going back. You'd have to find a way to get out of any mess you got yourself into. As hard as it was, it was great fun to be a part of the *AMC* gang.

They did take a time-out one day to spring a special surprise on me. I was in a scene in a bar with Myrtle when someone dressed in the cleaning lady outfit I always wore on my show made an entrance mopping the floor. She proceeded to bump into my chair. This wasn't in the script, so I jumped up, turned around, and heard this great big belly laugh coming out of her. The crew was howling. She took off the mop cap and there stood Elizabeth Taylor.

Elizabeth and I had worked together in an HBO movie,

Elizabeth and me on the set of Between Friends.

COURTESY OF CAROL BURNETT

Between Friends, earlier that year and had indeed become friends. Agnes had planned this surprise, and Elizabeth, being the good sport she is, donned the outfit and hid out in one of the dressing rooms all day until the time came for the gag. The cameras kept rolling, and her belly laugh and my expletive (bleeped) went on the air exactly as taped.

Keeping Up with Pine Valley While in Europe

*

Several years before I had my shining moment as Verla Grubbs, Joe and the girls and I went to Europe for four weeks during the summer. So as not to miss the Pine Valley goings-on, I had my friend Rick send me a telegram once a week cluing me in on the latest trials and tribulations of Erica and the gang. He had our itinerary, so every Friday I'd receive tidings from the concierge at our hotel in London, Paris, or Rome, keeping me up to date on my soap. I couldn't *wait* for those telegrams!

Our last stop was Lake Como in Italy, where we were going to connect with some family friends. We had driven from Rome and were pretty tired when we arrived. The hotel was quite beautiful, overlooking the vast lake. We had an early dinner with our friends, unpacked, and hit the sack. Around two in the morning, we were awakened by someone knocking on our door. The girls were sound asleep, so Joe and I threw on our robes, wondering what could be important enough to wake us at this hour. We opened the door and there stood our friends, also in their robes, looking ashen. The concierge had a telegram in his hand, which was shaking. I was encouraged to sit down.

Omigod, what's wrong? My friend put her arm around me. Joe stood there looking confused and grim. The concierge said, "*Signora*, I am so sorry," as he handed me the telegram.

```
CAROL: ERICA WAS KIDNAPPED AND HAS BEEN
FOUND IN A COMA. MARK SLIPPED AGAIN AND
RAN AWAY FROM REHAB. HE HASN'T BEEN FOUND.
MONA HAS TO HAVE EXPLORATORY SURGERY.
DOESN'T LOOK GOOD. CHUCK HAS LEARNED THAT
DONNA, WHO'S CARRYING HIS BABY, WAS ONCE A
HOOKER. DONNA'S HUSBAND, PALMER, IS STILL IN
THE DARK. THE WOMAN POSING AS BROOKE'S
MOTHER IS WANTED BY THE POLICE. PHOEBE IS
BACK ON THE BOTTLE. HOPE YOU'RE HAVING A
GREAT TRIP. LOVE, RICK
```

I started to laugh, which morphed into a kind of choking wail. I looked at everyone's worried expressions, and tears started running down my face. I was laughing so hard I couldn't speak. I'm sure everyone thought I was hysterical. They would have been right. The concierge suggested calling the house doctor, and my friends were all for it. Every time I tried to open my mouth to explain I burst into gales of laughter. Finally Joe took the telegram from me and read it. Then he started laughing, too.

"It's her soap."

They all turned their attention to Joe.

"Her *what*?"

I finally found my voice. Explanations and apologies filled the air.

After everybody had left and the lights were out again, I was still laughing as I drifted off to sleep.

I don't think that poor concierge ever got it.

Joan Crawford

I n the summer of 1962, I had my first contact with Joan
Crawford. I was touring with my own live variety show,
featuring the comedy team of Allen and Rossi and twenty
male dancers. We opened in Pittsburgh, and from there we played
theaters in Indianapolis, Kansas City, Dallas, and Detroit, closing
at the Sands Hotel in Las Vegas. *Variety* ran an article with a
headline saying that we broke records wherever we played.

When I got back to New York, there was a letter waiting
for me. It had been forwarded from my agent's office. The envelope was handwritten, and when I turned it over to look at the
back, there was a return address and a signature: "Joan Crawford." *Joan Crawford?*

I tore it open. The letter was also handwritten.

> *Darling Carol,*
>   *I've read with great interest of your highly
> successful tour this summer. Congratulations! I've
> been a fan of yours for a long time. It's always*

wonderful when good things happen to people
you love.

> *Sincerely, Joan*

I was dumbfounded. Joan Crawford. Wow. I remembered all the times my grandmother Nanny and I had sat weeping through a Joan Crawford drama. She was a queen.

I thought about answering her. I didn't want to seem forward, but I really wanted to express my gratitude for such a lovely letter.

> *Dear Miss Crawford,*
>   *Thank you so very much for your kind words.*
> *I was thrilled to hear from you. I'll save your letter*
> *forever!*
>   *Your fan, Carol Burnett*

A week went by. Another letter arrived.

> *Darling Carol,*
>   *I received your very sweet letter. And I'm*
> *planning on saving it the way you're saving mine.*
> *Hope all is well and I send you much love, and*
> *please, no more of this "Miss Crawford" crap!*
>   *Yours, Joan*

Should I write back? I wasn't sure what to do. Okay, I decided, one last time.

> *Dear Joan,*
>   *Thank you for asking me to call you Joan. I'm*
> *most honored. I hope to meet you in person someday.*
>   *With love, Carol*

The following week:

> *Darling Carol,*
> *I'm so glad you feel comfortable calling me*
> *Joan. I too hope we can meet in person someday!*
> *Life can be so short . . . but also wonderful. Don't*
> *you think so?*
>
> *Love, Joan*

I was at a loss. I didn't want to be rude, but I felt somewhat awkward having Joan Crawford as a pen pal.

I relayed this to a few other people in the business, and heard back that Joan Crawford wrote lots of letters to lots of people. I just couldn't figure out where she found the time.

I decided not to write anymore, hoping she'd still like me.

A couple of years later, Joe and I (now married) went to the Four Seasons restaurant in New York for dinner. It was a beautiful room, at the center of which was (and still is) a large lighted shallow pool, with tables surrounding it. While the maître d' was checking our reservation I looked around, and there at the nearest table, in a seat next to the pool, with three other folks, was . . . JOAN.

"Joe!" I whispered urgently. "There's Joan Crawford! What do we do?"

"What do you mean?"

"I never answered her last letter! Oh God, maybe she won't see us."

Looking straight ahead, we made it past her table. Then we heard her voice.

"Carol?"

We turned around. She stood up and reached across the table for my hand. I gave it to her.

"Hi, Miss Crawford."

"No, no, no! It's Joan!"

Introductions were made all around. She gave Joe and me a big hug. I felt better. She wasn't holding a grudge. We made our way across the room, where Joe and I were seated at a table for two next to the pool. The waiter handed out the menus. I glanced across the pool and saw Joan Crawford staring at me. I smiled and she blew me a kiss.

"Joe, she just blew me a kiss."

"Well, blow one back."

I did, and she blew another one.

"Joe, it's like the letters. We'll be blowing kisses all night."

Joe, ever the voice of reason, said, "Then don't look across the pool."

Right.

Dinner came and went, and I hadn't once glanced across the pool. I finally sneaked a peek and saw that her table was being cleared by a busboy. *Whew.*

I turned back to Joe and saw his eyes looking straight past my right shoulder and down at the floor. I turned around, and there was Joan Crawford next to my chair, on her knees.

"Carol darling, it's so wonderful to meet you in person after all these years."

"Thank you, Miss Crawford." I looked around. Nobody seemed to notice. "Please, get up."

She didn't. She just stayed there on the floor, on her knees. "No, no, no! It's Joan!"

"Joan . . . please, please, get up . . ."

"I'm fine right here." She wasn't budging. She took my hand and put it to her cheek. "I'm so happy for this evening!"

We told her that we were, too. Joe took her hand and helped her up. She gave him a dazzling smile.

Years later, on my variety show, we did a takeoff on *Mildred Pierce* (called "Mildred Fierce") after Joan Crawford had won an Oscar for the role. Bob Mackie had outfitted me in a pin-striped suit with enormous shoulder pads, which was a brilliant re-creation of her look in that movie. After our sketch aired, I got a letter from her: "I *loved* it. You gave it more production than that f——ing Jack Warner!"

Thus began another round of correspondence . . .

How Not to Make Small Talk with Royalty

*

Back in the 1970s the shah of Iran's sister and I had one thing in common: our obstetrician, Dr. Blake Watson. She flew all the way to California from Iran so he could deliver her babies. I drove from Beverly Hills to St. John's Hospital in Santa Monica, where he delivered my second and third: Jody in 1967 and Erin in 1968. (Carrie had been born in New York in 1963.) One day Dr. Watson called to invite Joe and me to a black-tie housewarming party that the shah of Iran's sister (the princess) was giving for herself. She had bought a home in Beverly Hills and had just finished redecorating it. Coincidentally, the house happened to be right up the street from our own, up a short and very steep hill that afforded her a spectacular view of the city. You could call us neighbors. Dr. Watson explained that the princess's children (who were now in their teens) watched our show whenever they were in the United States, and were fans. Hence the invitation.

The night of the party arrived, and Joe and I got all gussied up and drove up the hill. It took us about thirty seconds to get there.

A servant, formally dressed and wearing white gloves, opened the door, and we were ushered into a living room that looked like a Persian palace. Multi-colored beaded curtains divided the spacious rooms, thick area rugs lay on inlaid tile floors, and in place of sofas and chairs to sit on, there were huge silk pillows—burgundy, gold, jade, and deep purple, with their tassels combed out and spread neatly on the rugs. The room was empty. We were led out to the terrace, where guests were mingling and drinking champagne. Exotic languages filled the air.

We didn't recognize a soul. Everyone sounded and looked like they belonged in the UN. Over their tuxedo jackets some, of the men wore red sashes with a medal or two sewn on. The women looked like they had pilfered most of Queen Elizabeth's jewelry. A couple wore tiaras. In my black, long-sleeved turtleneck silk evening gown and pearl earrings, I was definitely underdressed. Joe, in his tux, looked swell. A gentleman (I think he was an aide of some sort) approached us and asked us to come and be introduced to our hostess.

She was lovely, with dark hair falling about her shoulders; she looked every inch a princess. After a few polite "How do you dos" she then turned her attention to more arriving guests. Joe and I stood there holding our champagne flutes and proceeded to make small talk . . . with each other.

"Carol! Joe!" At last—someone we knew! Dr. Watson and his wife made their way over. He had the princess's two teenagers in tow, and we were all introduced. The kids were shy, and it wasn't long before they were whisked away to meet other guests.

Cocktails dragged on for over an hour, and my feet were beginning to hurt. I turned to Joe. "If I don't get out of these heels soon, I'm going to faint. I *have* to sit down." Parting a beaded curtain, we wandered back into the living room and headed for the pillows. I gratefully plopped down on a big red number and promptly sank to the floor. Joe joined me. I slipped out of my shoes and stuck them under a couple of tassels. There we were, sitting side by side on these down-filled floor pillows, staring out into space, uncomfortable as all hell because there was nothing to lean against.

Then she appeared. The princess.

"May I join you?"

She sat down between us, and I swear *she* didn't sink to the floor. I couldn't figure it out. She had to have thighs of steel to support her legs like that. So there we sat, all three of us facing the same direction, looking like we were waiting for a bus. She towered over us.

Silence. I leaned back a little and looked around the princess at Joe, trying to make eye contact. He was staring straight ahead, and it didn't look like he was going to start up any kind of conversation anytime soon.

It was up to me.

CAROL: Soooo, Princess . . .
PRINCESS: *(looking down at me)* Yes?
CAROL: Y'know, we're neighbors. . . .
PRINCESS: Really?
CAROL: Yep. Sure are.

She smiled, nodded, and faced front again.
Silence.

CAROL: Yessireebob, we're just right down there at
            the foot of this hill—spitting distance, you

might say. Yep, right at the foot of this very same hill.

Joe coughed. The tone of his cough carried a touch of warning, but I barreled on.

CAROL: Sooo . . . gosh, the next time you're in town . . . well, hey, why don't you just roll on down the hill for a bowl of Rice Krispies?

I couldn't believe that had come out of my mouth.

PRINCESS: Rice Krispies?

Joe cleared his throat. No use. Too late.

CAROL: Uh, you know . . . Snap, Crackle, and Pop?

She stood up, thanked me for the invitation, and made a beeline for the terrace.

I've been a Cheerios person ever since.

Stanwyck and the
Leprechaun

*

The year was 1981 and I was in the middle of a trial. I was suing the *National Enquirer* for printing a false story that I had been romping around drunk in a Washington, D.C., restaurant, forcing desserts down customers' throats and winding up in a fight with Henry Kissinger. The whole story was made up, except for the fact that Dr. Kissinger and I happened to be dining there that same evening, at separate tables. Period.

I had been advised at the time to just let it go because the next morning the article would be lining birdcages. But I didn't want to let it go. Nobody was going to lie about me like that and think they could get away with it. It took five long years to get to the point of a jury trial, at which time we were able to prove that the *Enquirer* had made the whole thing up, and I was awarded a hefty sum. I paid my lawyers and donated the rest of the money to various schools promoting ethics in journalism.

While I was still in the middle of the trial, I had an early appointment with my doctor for a quick checkup before heading downtown to the courthouse for another long day of testimony and long-winded lawyers. Dog-tired of the whole thing, I was beginning to wish I *had* let it go.

I sat down in my doctor's waiting room and picked up a year-old magazine. As I was flipping through the pages, the door opened and in walked Barbara Stanwyck, a major movie star for over fifty years—and one of my idols. We didn't know each other, so I tried not to be intrusive and kept my eyes glued to *Popular Mechanics*. One thing about my doctor—he never dropped the names of his other patients.

Barbara Stanwyck sat down on the couch across the room and started rummaging through her purse. I peeked over at her. She looked wonderful. She was in her seventies, and her strong face was framed by a beautiful head of snow-white hair. She was wearing a smart black suit with a diamond pin on the lapel, and her still shapely legs were crossed at the ankles. She found her glasses and put them on. She looked at me and smiled. I nodded and smiled back.

She spoke first. "I have something to tell you."

Usually that meant a conversation about our TV variety show.

"Yes?"

"You're going to whip the *Enquirer*'s ass."

I laughed. "Miss Stanwyck, from your lips to God's ears."

"Don't laugh. It's a done deal, so you can just relax. Trust me."

"Boy, that would be great. Thanks so much for your encouragement."

She flashed those eyes, and I got the feeling that she was somewhat agitated with me.

"Look, I'm not making this up or wishing you the best here, get it? I'm telling you I KNOW you're gonna win this case."

I didn't know how to respond. I sure didn't feel like disagreeing with Barbara Stanwyck.

She leaned forward and, almost in a whisper, said, "My leprechaun told me."

I smiled, nodded, and for once in my life I kept quiet.

"Oh, they exist, all right. I have this one who's *never* wrong. He's seen me through thick and thin. And he told me Carol Burnett's going to whip their ass."

The receptionist opened the door. "You can come in now, Miss Stanwyck."

Before she disappeared into the doctor's office, she looked back at me and smiled. "Don't forget now—he's never wrong." She held up two fingers and said, "Now, number one, get a good night's sleep. Number two, remember their ass is gonna get whipped."

I did.

And it was.

A Girl Named Kathy

*

We were just about ready to wrap up our eighth season in March 1975. It was our next-to-last week. I remember that Phil Silvers (of *Sgt. Bilko* fame) and Jean Stapleton (Edith on *All in the Family*) were our guest stars. It was Monday. We had just finished rehearsing and I was in my office getting ready to go home. Joe was working in his office with the writers and would join me later. I picked up my script, said goodnight to my secretary, Rae Whitney, and headed down the hall for the elevator. I pressed the down button and waited. Just as the doors started to open, Rae came running down the hall.

"Wait!"

"What is it?"

"You just got a call from a woman who would like you to phone her twelve-year-old daughter who's in the hospital, dying of cancer. I wanted to give you the number, in case you'd want to call."

She gave me the phone number of the hospital room and I entered the elevator.

I got home and went upstairs to the small room off the bedroom where I kept a writing desk, stationery, pens, and a telephone. Reading the number Rae had given me, I found myself on the fence as to whether I should call or not. How should I sound? Upbeat? Sympathetic? I wasn't sure what to do. I had always avoided requests like this because I never knew how to handle them. Sometimes I sent balloons or flowers, but I never got *close.*

And yet . . . this was different. I didn't know why, but suddenly I knew I had to make the call.

The phone rang on the other end of the line. A woman picked it up.

"Hello?"

"Hi. This is Carol Burnett, and I got a message to call Kathy."

"Omigod! Thank you so much. This is Kathy's mom, Paula."

"Hi, Paula."

"I can't begin to tell you how much this will mean to her. She has been watching your show ever since she was a baby."

"Is Kathy available to talk?"

"Oh my, yes! She's right here."

I heard her whisper something. There was a bit of a pause, and then: "Hello?" The voice was faint and thin.

"Kathy?"

"Yes."

"Hi, dear. This is Carol. I got your message to call. I hope this is a good time for you?"

"Yes."

"Your mom tells me you watch our show all the time."

"Yes."

"Do you have any favorite parts?"

"I like it when Tim makes Harvey laugh, and when you're the dumb secretary."

"Mrs. Wiggins?"

"Yes." She sounded breathy at this point, like talking was becoming too much of an effort. I had an idea.

"Kathy, can I talk to your mom?"

Paula came to the phone. "Thank you so much. Kathy's thrilled."

I asked her if Kathy was up to any kind of travel. "You see, we have a run-through of the show at three o'clock every Wednesday afternoon in a rehearsal hall at CBS—for the writers and the crew—and I was wondering if you could find out from Kathy's doctor if it would be okay for her to attend. I could send a car to bring you and take you back. Do you think it would be possible?"

The doctor made it possible.

It was time for our Wednesday run-through. We were all gathered in the rehearsal hall getting ready to go through the week's sketches and musical numbers. I kept looking at the door. It finally opened and there she was, along with her mother, Paula. Kathy was in a wheelchair. She was so very thin. She was bald. I ran over to them, hugged Paula, and bent down to give Kathy a kiss, but I could tell something else was wrong. She was blind. Paula explained that it had happened just the day before.

I had only known about Kathy for two days, but I felt my heart breaking. I couldn't take my eyes off her beautiful little face. I kissed her and put her hands to my cheeks. Her fingers traced my features. I did my best to keep from crying. I didn't want her to feel the tears that were welling up. Yet here was this extraordinary child, actually *smiling*. I put her hands in mine and felt a most strange sensation, not unlike a small jolt of electricity: *I know this child. I have been with her before, somewhere, somehow.*

Joe came over, and I introduced him to Paula and Kathy. He was visibly shaken.

Then it was time for the run-through.

After a typical Wednesday rehearsal I would go upstairs to meet with Joe and the writers and talk about any changes we needed to make. This time I told Joe I was going to stay in the rehearsal hall and visit with Kathy and her mom before it was time to get them back to the hospital. Joe wasn't pleased, but he understood how I felt, and left me with them.

Paula told me that ever since Kathy was four and our show was on, she would walk over to the TV, point to me, and say, "That lady's my friend . . . my friend!"

All I could think was, *I know, I know.*

She also said that Kathy was resigned to her fate. She told me that after she went bald as a result of chemotherapy, they were at the beach one day and some kids had teased her because of her lack of hair. Paula had chased them away, clearly upset. Kathy told her mother it was okay. "I'm not supposed to be here long. I've always known it. It's okay."

I walked them down to the waiting car and asked Paula to call me when they got back to the hospital to let me know how Kathy had held up.

She called around dinnertime. "Kathy's temperature went up slightly, but she's been smiling and telling all the nurses what an exciting time she had. The doctor said it was good medicine."

Thursday was camera blocking and music day. I couldn't get Kathy out of my head (heart?). That night I went into my little office and put pen to paper.

> *Dearest Kathy,*
> *I feel that I've known you before. Your mom*
> *told me that you've always felt a connection between*
> *us. I can believe it, because I felt the same way in the*

deepest part of my very soul the minute we met.
Remember this: If you need me to be with you
whenever the time comes, let me know and I'll be
there with you. Don't forget. I'll be there, Kathy.

All my love,
Your friend, Carol

I folded the paper and tucked it away in a small drawer in my desk, knowing I would never mail it. I simply wanted to write my thoughts down and put them out there in the universe. It felt good.

On Friday we taped the show, and at the beginning, when I did the question-and-answer segment, I said hello to Kathy, which was my way of dedicating the show to her.

On the drive home that night Joe expressed his feelings about Kathy. He was worried that I was getting too close and might get hurt. I told him I couldn't help it, that there was much, much more to this experience than met the eye. I said I didn't know when it would be over but I was in it for the long haul—that much I knew. I also knew I wouldn't get hurt. I felt that, somehow, this was one of the most important events of my life, and I should meet it head-on.

I talked to Paula on Sunday, and she said Kathy had been sleeping a lot but seemed to be comfortable.

We were all back at work Monday for our final week of the season. Had it only been one week since Rae had given me Paula's phone message?

Ken and Mitzie Welch had put together a lovely medley of lullabies for Vicki and me to sing that week, ending with the familiar song "Lullaby and Goodnight." I said I wanted us to sing it into a tape recorder so I could send it to Kathy in the hospital. After we taped it, I called Paula to tell her I was sending, via a limo service, the tape and the recorder down to the hospital for

Kathy to listen to. That night she called me at home and said she had put the recorder on Kathy's pillow and that she had been listening to the medley all day.

We rehearsed the show all day on Tuesday. I was having trouble concentrating. That night at home I couldn't eat anything. The weirdest feelings started to come over me. I actually felt my insides vibrating. Joe and I put our girls to bed, and I decided to turn in early.

I was still awake when Joe came to bed later, but I pretended to be asleep. I didn't want him to know how revved up I was. All night my mind kept racing with the words, *Hang on, Kathy . . . hang on, Kathy . . . hang on, hang on, hang on, hang on, please hang on.* I must have drifted off at some point, but I was still begging Kathy to hang on when I looked at the clock at five in the morning.

Joe got up at eight and went to the office. Today was Wednesday, run-through day, one week to the day since I had met Kathy. My usual Wednesday began with costume fittings with Bob Mackie at ten, but I knew what I had to do. I had to drive down to the hospital to be with Kathy.

I called our associate producer, Bob Wright, and told him I wouldn't be going to Mackie's or rehearsing that day, but I assured him I'd be back in time for the three o'clock run-through, and we could fit costumes after that. Bob was concerned, and I asked him to please tell Joe and everyone else not to worry.

I left the house at ten. It would be a two-hour drive to the hospital. All the way down in the car, I kept talking to Kathy. Suddenly I felt an enormous *presence* in the car with me. I was not alone. And again my insides started to vibrate . . .

I got to the hospital at noon, ran into the waiting room area, and saw Paula there with her parents. Paula hugged me. "I knew you'd be here." She introduced me to Kathy's grandparents. I told Paula I could only stay until 1:00 because I had to be back for the run-through by 3:00. She took me down the hall to Kathy. I learned that she had slipped into a coma the night before. Kathy was in the ICU, hooked up to all kinds of tubes. I sat down beside her bed and held her hand. The tape recorder was lying on the pillow next to her ear. Paula pressed the play button and I could hear Vicki and me singing the medley.

"She's been listening to it ever since it arrived. I know she can hear it now." We sat there quietly for a while. I looked at the clock on the wall: twelve-thirty. Since the ICU would let only two people in the room at a time, when Paula brought her parents in, she and I went out into the hall. I told her that I had written a letter to Kathy and that even though I hadn't actually sent it, I felt she must've known what I had written, because of the overwhelming feelings that had engulfed me all night and in the car driving down.

I have always believed there is something more to this world than just us. I remember being four years old and lying on the grass in the backyard in San Antonio looking up at the clouds. I don't know how much time passed before I felt my body merging with the sky and the ground. *I was everything, and everything was me.*

Things had come my way over the years that I didn't exactly pray for but which had come to me in a sort of vision. I'd seen myself on campus at UCLA, and it happened. I'd seen myself living in New York, and it happened. I'd seen myself performing on Broadway for director George Abbott, and it happened. I always felt that I was somehow being looked after, that there was a Higher Power in and around all of us.

I saw myself being needed by Kathy and I wanted to embrace the connection between us.

I said to Paula, "I had to come."

"I know."

Kathy's grandparents joined us in the hall for a couple of

minutes before Paula and I went back into the room. I would have to leave very soon, even though I didn't want to.

Paula and I sat on each side of the bed and held her daughter's hands. The tape recorder was playing softly. It got to the end, "Lullaby and Goodnight," and Kathy breathed a long sigh. She was gone. I looked at the clock.

It was 1:00.

Higher Power filled the room.

The End of the Run

*

At the end of our tenth season, ABC offered Harvey a chance to star in his own sitcom. We knew we'd miss him like crazy, but it was an offer he couldn't (and shouldn't) refuse.

During the decade that we'd worked together, the network had moved our show around a lot. We'd started out on Mondays, were moved to Wednesdays (where we did poorly at eight-thirty), and then hit our stride on Saturdays at ten following *All in the Family*, *M*A*S*H*, *Mary Tyler Moore*, and *Bob Newhart*. Years later we were moved yet again, this time to Sundays.

Our eleventh year went well enough. Tim and Vicki were still on board, and we had some terrific guests to help fill the huge hole that Harvey left: Dick Van Dyke, Ken Berry, Steve Lawrence, and James Garner, to name a few. Once again Jim Nabors was our first guest at the beginning of the season. Our good-luck charm was still working, but change was in the air.

Even though CBS asked us to come back for a twelfth season, I felt that it was time to hang it up. This was not an easy

Tim, me, Harvey, and Vicki (our tenth season).

decision by any means. But we had put on 280 shows, which involved roughly 2,520 sketches and musical elements. We were starting to repeat ourselves in some instances, and I had always felt that it was a good idea to leave a party before the host starts to turn off the lights.

The last show was bittersweet. It was 1978 and our creative family had been through so much together over the years: marriages, divorces, births, deaths, bad times, and good times. We were all blubbering when the final strains of "I'm So Glad We Had This Time Together" were being played. I sang, "Comes the time we have to say so long," pulled my ear for the last time, and it was all over.

We had a blast of a party that night. Laughter and tears flowed like champagne. So did the champagne.

Several years later, sadly, Joe and I parted. The marriage was over, but we would always be friends.

He died in 1991 after a long and brave struggle with cancer.

Annie *and* John Huston

*

In 1981 I got a call from producer Ray Stark, asking me to play Miss Hannigan in the film version of the Broadway hit musical *Annie*. I jumped at the chance. The girls and I had been spending a lot of time in Hawaii, and I think I might've been suffering from island fever. Besides, I had never had the good fortune of being in a movie musical, and the idea of it thrilled me, especially when I heard that my friend Bernadette Peters was going to play Lily, along with Tim Curry (star of *The Rocky Horror Picture Show*) as Rooster, and the brilliant actor Albert Finney as Daddy Warbucks. The producers had conducted a massive talent search and discovered the adorable ten-year-old Aileen Quinn to play Annie. To top it all off, the movie was to be directed by the one and only John Huston.

John Huston rarely did more than two takes for a scene. He knew what he wanted, got it, and that was that. My kind of guy. He made the ladies feel very special, too. I'd never had my hand kissed before, and I'll never forget it. He also wanted his actors to have fun experimenting during rehearsals. He was definitely an actor's director!

My very first day I asked him for direction in the scene I was about to do. He simply said, "Cavort, dear, just cavort." *Okay. Got it. He hired me to cavort, so I'll cavort away.*

After a few days of shooting, some of us felt that the movie was being overproduced. Although Mr. Huston was always graciously encouraging his actors to discuss how to play a scene, it wasn't our place to make any comments to our director on our feelings about producer Ray Stark's production values or how he wanted to spend his money. Personally, I think Mr. Huston was interested in the more intimate scenes rather than in the extravagant musical numbers being choreographed by Broadway veteran Joe Layton.

However, because of my television training, I couldn't get over the huge amount of money that was being lavished on the street set. Along with Annie's orphanage, Easy Street was home to dozens of storefronts and old town houses complete with fire escapes. There were fishmongers with pushcarts, selling fish wrapped in old newspapers. There was an organ-grinder with a scary spider monkey sporting eyelashes, lipstick, and long red-painted fingernails. There were stores selling old clothes, dolls, and dishes. There were pawnshops galore. It was a monumentally beautiful set that (in my mind, anyway) could've cost a lot less than the many, many thousands of dollars being spent.

Okay, maybe none of the above sounds overboard, but consider that the fish wrapped in old newspapers were *real fish.* Only the tails stuck out, and you really couldn't even see them in the final shot. As far as I was concerned, at most all they needed was a fake rubber tail sticking out, for cryin' out loud. (I don't know how much money that would've saved, but it sure would have cut down on the smell.)

I took a look in the windows of the faux pawnshops and saw dozens, no, dozens and *dozens* of authentic pieces of antique jewelry and watches on display, which you also couldn't see in any of the shots. The porcelain dolls were collectibles. What was *that* all about? You never saw any of this in the final movie.

Then it came time to shoot the "Easy Street" number. In the original Broadway show the number featured only Hannigan, Rooster, and Lily, all thrilled about finding the other half of Annie's locket, which would put them on Easy Street for the rest of their lives. The number took place in a room in the orphanage with only the three characters. It was simple, and it had been a showstopper onstage.

Now here comes the movie version. With its four hundred dancers, "Easy Street" rehearsed for weeks. We swung and climbed on the fire escapes. We danced up the street. We danced down the street. With all these dancers, the original intent of the number was completely lost—the whole thing looked like a big bucket of worms. As far as I could tell, there was no point being made other than BIG.

We had to call a halt for a while because the monkey with the nails dug them into my underarm and I had to hit the studio nurse's office for a tetanus shot. (I hated that monkey.) Bernadette, Tim, and I just shook our heads and soldiered on. This number was going nowhere, and if I wasn't mistaken, it was costing upward of a million dollars.

The filming was over. Mr. Huston kissed my hand and we gave each other a big hug. We all said our goodbyes and headed home: me to Maui, Bernadette to New York, and Tim to England.

Once I was back in Hawaii, I decided to go for something special: a chin.

I had always wanted a chin. I was born with a weak one, which may explain why I went into comedy. I remember the wonderful comedy writer Larry Gelbart saying in some article,

John Huston and me, as Miss Hannigan, on the set of Annie.

COURTESY OF CAROL BURNETT

"Carol Burnett is almost very pretty." And I remember being quoted as replying, "That was almost very nice of him."

Anyhow, now I had a chin, thanks to an oral surgeon in Honolulu who had corrected the problem. Even though I still wasn't very pretty, I was very thrilled. I could feel the Maui rain on my chin without having to look up. It wasn't a huge difference (three millimeters, to be precise), but it made a big difference to me.

The phone rang. It was Ray Stark calling from California. "We're going to re-shoot 'Easy Street' with just the three of you: Bernadette, Tim, and you. It'll be so much better this way."

Yep. Agreed. But why didn't they think of this in the first place?

"Um . . . there's one little problem, Ray. I have a chin."

"What?"

"I have a new chin. Oral surgery. I was operated on a month ago in Honolulu. The doctor added about three millimeters, and . . . ah . . . gosh, it might be noticeable."

Slight pause. "No problem. There won't be any scenes where we go from close-up to close-up. No one will notice a thing. Plus, you're in all that costume and makeup. There'll be a lot of scenes in between. Nobody's gonna be lookin' at your chin, trust me."

Okay by me.

It was great to be reunited with Tim and Bernadette and Mr. Huston. *And* it was great to know that they had decided to scrap the "Easy Street" four-hundred-dancer debacle and simplify the number, with all of it taking place inside the orphanage.

We were getting ready for the first shot when Mr. Huston said: "All right. I want to back up the scene a little and pick it up where Carol comes out of the closet waving the locket."

I approached him cautiously.

"Mr. Huston?"

"Carol, when are you going to call me John?"

"Uh . . . John . . . excuse me, but two months ago, when we shot this scene, I went into the closet with *no chin*, and now I'm coming out of the closet *with* a chin. I just want to call that to your attention."

He thought for a moment and then said, "All right then, dear. Just come out looking *determined*."

Turbulence

*

I've never been crazy about flying. I do it, but I'm not crazy about it. But I *am* crazy about Harry Connick Jr., so when I was invited to his wedding to Jill Goodacre in 1994 (I was also friends with Jill's mother, Glenna), I booked a first-class flight to New Orleans, Harry's hometown, where they were to be married.

I boarded the plane and found my aisle seat. I like the aisle seat because if I have to get up for any reason, I don't have to crawl over a stranger. I had my crossword puzzles with me and was all set. When I looked around, I was surprised to see that I was the only one seated in the first-class cabin. I asked the flight attendant about it, and she said they were waiting for a bus to unload the rest of the passengers due for this flight.

They finally arrived—all young Japanese businessmen, in suits and ties, carrying briefcases—and suddenly I was the only one in first class who wasn't a young Japanese businessman. My window seat partner scooted in, sat down, and put his brief-case under the seat in front of him. I glanced at him. He stared straight ahead. There was lots of talking before we taxied, all in Japanese. Once we were airborne, my fellow passenger opened up his computer, and I was up to my ears in *New York Times* crossword puzzle torture. I looked around the cabin and they *all* had their computers lit up and were clicking away.

The flight attendant served drinks. Occasionally I looked over at my seat companion, but he made no effort at communication; it's not that I particularly wanted any, but sometimes it's nice to acknowledge the presence of another human being. He was buried in his work. *Oh well.* I went back to trying to come up with a four-letter word for "homologous."

Then came a sort of bump. My drink bounced a little on the tray. As I said, I don't like flying, and I *definitely* don't like bumps. Nobody else seemed to notice, though. The flight became smooth again.

Lunch was served.

Then there was a lurch. The plane *lurched.* Lunch started to slip from side to side on the tray. *Whoa . . .*

The flight attendants took away our lurching lunches.

"Ladies and gentlemen, we have some slight turbulence ahead, due to the weather conditions in this part of the country. Please fasten your seat belts."

I looked at my seat partner. He had closed up his computer. I folded up my puzzle and tightened my seat belt.

Another lurch sent the flight attendant flying up to the ceiling and back, almost landing in my lap. Not a good sign. The captain asked the flight attendants to take their seats and buckle up. Another bad sign.

Then the plane started to go up and down. *Way* up and *way* down. I looked at the flight attendant who sat facing the cabin, buckled up in her seat. Her face was without expression—or color. I knew she was scared out of her wits, along with the rest of us. The wings began to tip this way and that, and the plane began making creaking noises.

There was screaming coming from the back of the plane, but up front we were strangely silent. All the young Japanese businessmen were staring straight ahead, quiet as hell.

The next thing I knew, we had gone into a steep nosedive. The noise was horrific. I figured we'd bought the farm. We were going down. It occurred to me that the young man I was sitting next to would be the last human face I'd ever see, the last human being I'd ever touch. I reached over and squeezed his hand. He squeezed back, and then turned and looked at me for the first time since we took off.

Our eyes locked. I smiled weakly, and what came out of my mouth was "Sayonara."

Obviously, we survived.

Living in a High-Rise
All Alone

*

I n the early 1980s the girls and I decided to move back from Hawaii to the mainland and re-settle in Los Angeles. Joe was there, and we wanted the girls to be closer to him. Since he was living in an apartment on Wilshire Boulevard, I looked in that area and was able to find a two-bedroom place on the eighteenth floor in a brand-new high-rise called the Wilshire House, a few blocks away from Joe's building.

At that time "the Corridor," as Wilshire Boulevard is often called, had a lot of construction going on. Apartment buildings were springing up all over the place, but not too many people were buying. In fact, the girls and I were the first and for a time the *only* residents of the Wilshire House. Living there could've been the basis for a sitcom. There I was, with no neighbors, six valet parking attendants, Chauncey the handyman, and Ruth the telephone operator.

Friends would phone, and Ruth would answer, "The Wilshire House, how may I help you?"

The reply would be, "Is she home?"

Jody, Carrie, and Erin.
COURTESY OF CAROL BURNETT

Mine would be the only apartment lit up at night.

When I got into the elevator, it was always an express.

The parking attendants fought over who would open my car door, just so they could have something to do.

Chauncey was always asking me if my pilot light and faucets

were okay because, like the valets, he didn't have much to do, either.

In a peculiar way, we were a family of sorts.

The following Christmas the girls and I spent two weeks in Honolulu. When I returned, Chauncey was helping me with my luggage, and as we got into the express elevator he said, "It's sure good to have you back, Miz B. Ya know, the old place just wasn't the same without you."

We lived there like that for one whole year.

When other people started moving in, we moved out. That was purely a coincidence, but it always struck me as funny.

Body by Jake

*

At age fourteen my daughter Erin was attending a rather progressive school in Santa Monica, California. It struck me as progressive because the students were encouraged to call their teachers by their first names, the classes allowed a lot of cross talk, and there was no particular dress code. I'm not sure, but I think the kids sometimes went barefoot. Being a product of high school in the 1950s, I always felt it was a little *too* casual.

I attended a parent-teacher meeting where I was introduced to the very good-looking headmaster (by our first names). I aired my reservations to him, probably sounding slightly prudish, and he assured me that my fears were unfounded, although he added that I wasn't the only parent who had expressed those concerns. He also asked if I would be willing to help host a banquet they held every fall. I told him to be sure to call me when the time was nearer, as I wasn't sure of my schedule.

The school seemed to have it pretty much together curriculum-wise, and Erin was happy there, so after a while I felt a little better. I attended some of the school plays. The acting was what you'd expect from a group of junior high school kids, yet I couldn't get over how grown-up these teenagers looked onstage. They spared no makeup, but happily they were up on how to apply it, thanks to the media and fashion magazines. I took a friend to one of the student musicals, and his comment was, "They look divorced."

Still, Erin's grades remained pretty good and she continued to enjoy going to school with a lot of kids she had grown up with, so who was I to cause problems?

A few weeks later, I decided I needed to work on my fitness. Hating to exercise on my own, I knew I needed help to get me jump-started. There was a trainer in LA famous for making house calls and getting people off their behinds. His name was Jake, and his company was called *Body by Jake.* A few of my friends had hired him as their trainer and swore by him. So I called his office and left my phone number, my name, and a message asking if he might make some time for me and arrange a workout schedule.

A few days later, my phone rang.

"Hello?"

"Carol?"

"Yes."

"This is Jake."

"Hi, Jake. So what are we going to do about my body?"

There was a slight pause, and then "Excuse me?"

"You have to help me out here, Jake. My body needs *major attention!*"

I heard him clear his throat, followed by a longer pause. It was then that the penny dropped. I realized I was talking to

Erin's headmaster, whose first name also happened to be . . . you guessed it!

I started to attempt to explain the mix-up to Jake the headmaster but found myself starting to howl with laughter. He said he'd call back later.

He never did.

Dating

*

It felt weird to even *think* of dating again at my age: forty-nine! It was even harder after I started dating, because I reverted to being a teenager whenever someone called to ask me out. I even grew a few zits just thinking about it. I was quite simply out of practice. I was much more comfortable going out with friends, or taking one of my girls—or all three—with me to a function. But I knew I had to stay with it or I could wind up being a hermit, and worse, *liking* it.

So one night I had dinner in Beverly Hills with a very nice and attractive man whom I had known for a while in a professional capacity. The evening was pleasant enough but slightly strained. There were l-o-n-g pauses in the conversation. I was beginning to regret having accepted the invitation. We really didn't have that much in common. As he was driving me home, all I could think about was: *What if he expects me to invite him in? Do I offer him a drink? What'll we talk about? How long would he stay? What if he wants a goodnight kiss?*

I was beginning to feel a small anxiety attack coming on. As we were pulling up to my front door I said: "Thanks so much! Don't bother to stop. Just slow down and I'll jump out here." I hit the ground running, whirled around, smiled, and waved goodbye. Just another benefit of a body by Jake.

Marlon Brando

*

In the mid-eighties I spent some time in New York, writing a memoir for my daughters about growing up. I stayed at the Wyndham Hotel. The Wyndham was known as the actors' hotel, since lots of people appearing in Broadway shows chose the warmth and coziness of the Wyndham over more modern hotels. Some folks, like Hume Cronyn and Jessica Tandy, made it their permanent New York City residence. The rooms had Old World charm. The bathrooms were the size of a postage stamp, and sometimes the water pressure and temperature left a lot to be desired. The telephone system was antiquated: a switchboard, Rose the operator, and a desk.

Sometimes you'd have to wait several minutes before Rose could get around to your call. But the staff—and owners Suzanne and John Mados—more than made up for any shortcomings. If it was cold outside, the elevator operator, Mohammed, would always make sure I had the right kind of clothing on before he would let me out in the lobby. "Please go back and put on a warmer coat, Miss Burnett, it's pretty cold out there today." It was like living in a big boardinghouse where everybody looked out for each other.

On this day I had been out all afternoon and was looking forward to spending a quiet evening in my room. Rose handed me some messages on little pink slips.

"You got one there from Marlon Brando."

"What?"

"Yep. Brando."

I looked at the message: "Marlon Brando would like to talk to you. Please call." There was a Los Angeles number.

I said, "This has to be some kind of joke. I don't know Marlon Brando"—*though I'd love to.*

"Nope. No joke. Recognized the voice."

All the way up in the elevator I stared at the message slip. *Marlon Brando? If this isn't a joke of some kind, what on earth would he want with me?*

I threw my purse on the bed, sat down, and picked up the phone without removing my coat.

Rose picked up. "Got it." She was already dialing his number.

It was three hours earlier in California—2:15 P.M., to be exact.

He picked up on the first ring. "Hello?"

"Mr. Brando?"

"Who's this?"

No mistaking that voice. "Hi. It's Carol Burnett. You left a message for me to call?"

"Yeah, your agent told me how to find you. Thanks for calling back."

"You're welcome."

"Where'd you get your chin?"

"My chin?"

"Yeah, where'd ya get it? I remember reading the interview you gave about it—was it in *People?*"

He's calling about my *chin.*

"You see, my wife's sister has a weak chin and wants to fix it. Where'd you get yours done?"

"In Honolulu . . . about two years ago."

"Did it hurt?"

"No. Not really."

"They have to break your jaw?"

"Not in my case. He only added three millimeters—"

"Hang on. Lemme get a pencil."

I heard him walking away and opening a drawer. *Omigod, I'm talking to Marlon Brando.* He came back to the phone. "Mind giving me the doctor's name and number?"

Now *I* had to walk away and open a drawer. I found my address book and went back into the bedroom and sat back down on the bed. I still had on my coat. Suddenly I got the urge to go to the bathroom. I gave him the necessary information. I had to repeat it a couple of times so he could get it right. I also had to pee.

He thanked me, and then said, "So, did you have fun all those years?"

"You mean our television show?"

"Yeah. You guys had a lot to learn every week. What kind of schedule were you on?"

I told him what our schedule was, and he seemed pretty impressed that our working hours were decent. He asked about the costuming. "Some of those outfits were pretty amazing."

I explained that Bob Mackie was the genius behind every piece of clothing we wore.

"Did he come up with that *Gone With the Wind* getup?"

"Yep. He sure did!" I was starting to squirm. The urge hadn't passed. I started eyeing the bathroom door.

Then he got on the subject of comedy. "So, how much dif-ferent is it, doing it in front of an audience instead of a single camera on a movie set? It's gotta affect your timing, right?"

I couldn't believe it. Marlon Brando was asking *me* about comedy technique. I stood up and started pacing around the foot of the bed. By this time I was perspiring. My poor bladder was begging, *pleading* for relief. The bathroom was only a few short feet away. Would the phone cord be long enough to reach? And even if it did reach, would he hear what I was doing?

It didn't reach, so that took care of that. It was back to pac-ing and sweating. I didn't have the nerve to share my plight with him. What if he hung up?

"So, how'd you guys do it week after week?"

I mean, how often do you get a call from someone like him? To me, this was momentous, gargantuan . . . something I'd tell my grandchildren someday. ("Let me tell you the story about how Marlon Brando asked me about *my* thoughts on comedy.")

The subject somehow switched to our childhoods. He talked about his upbringing and asked about mine. He was telling me personal stories, stories that he said he wanted to write about someday. Amazing revelations. I told him I was halfway through a memoir, and he asked me how I'd gotten started. Here he was opening up to me, asking me all these questions, and *I had to pee*.

The time passed *slowly*. I was in heaven and hell at the same time.

I looked at the clock. We had been talking for over an hour.

I thought I'd go out of my mind. If this went on much longer, I would quite simply explode and be dead. Finally: "Mr. Brando?"

"Marlon."

"Thank you . . . uh . . . gosh, I'm sorry, but my other phone line is lit up and I'm expecting a call from my daughter."

"Oh, sure. Well, thanks so much."

"Thank *you*! And I hope it works out with your sister-in-law's chin."

We hung up, and I just made it.

The phone started to ring while I was still in the bathroom. It kept ringing. When I finally picked it up, Rose said, *"What other line?"*

Mr. Computer

*

When I was writing *One More Time* back in 1985, I was afraid I'd miss the deadline that the book publisher, Random House, had given me. I had fallen way behind. The problem was that I had started writing in longhand on yellow legal pads and then I'd copy the pages onto a typewriter. Several times I would look at a finished typewritten page and wish I could move some paragraphs and sentences around to see if they would read better. So I'd get out the old scissors and paste, manually cutting out the paragraphs or sentences I wanted to move and pasting them elsewhere. Sometimes an hour or more would go by and I'd still be fiddling with that one sticky page. At that rate I knew I'd never finish.

A friend suggested a computer. That way I could move words, sentences, and paragraphs around in a matter of seconds and not waste so much time.

A COMPUTER? ME? Dear Lord, no. I couldn't possibly! I just wasn't mechanically inclined. But after a lot more cutting and pasting, I realized I'd have to bite the bullet.

That same friend recommended the computer store she'd bought hers from: Friendly Computers, in Santa Monica. I was comforted by the name, but walking into the store was somewhat daunting. Surrounded by all those machines and screens made me feel like I was in the middle of some kind of spaceship. I was about to run out the door when a little girl approached me.

"Can I help you?"

Close up she wasn't a little girl, just a young woman who looked like a twelve-year-old.

"Um . . . I . . . I . . ." I finally got up the courage and blurted out, "I'm afraid I need a computer, but I don't know what kind."

"Do you know what you need it for?"

"I'm trying to write a book."

I wound up buying this large *thing* that came not only with a detailed (and utterly confusing) instruction book, which had some very nice drawings in it, but also with a series of hour-long one-on-one instruction sessions given by the little girl, whose name turned out to be Beth.

We set a date for delivery and I left the store feeling like a dinosaur.

The delivery date came, and I found myself dreading the *bing-bong* of my doorbell. . . .

Bing-bong.

I opened the door and there was Beth, completely hidden behind the large thing she was holding. All I could see was her feet. I showed her to my desk, and she said it would take a few minutes to set everything up (including a printer with rolls of sprocket-feed paper that came with the whole shebang). She was done in no time.

Raring to go, she said, "Okay! C'mon, sit down. Let's get going!"

"Uh, Beth, would you like a glass of water? Do you need to go to the bathroom or something? Are you hungry?"

Smiling, she shook her head, patted my chair, and sweetly said, "Sit."

I sat and stared at the blank screen. I was scared. I mean *scared*.

"Beth, I'm going to say something now that might sound a little silly to you, but here goes . . . I know absolutely nothing about computers, so *please* treat me as if I'm a three-year-old in a sandbox."

"That's not silly at all. Are you ready?"

I gulped and nodded.

She began to explain, pointing at and patting the machine as she spoke. "Now, this is Mr. Computer. When we want Mr. Computer to light up, what do we do? Why, we press Mr. On Button. When we want Mr. Computer to go night-night, we press Mr. Off Button."

And so it went. The hour flew by, and when it was over, I was able to type and move sentences and paragraphs all over the place like a pro. We set another instruction date, and as I showed her to the door I said, "Beth, you're not only the best teacher I've ever had, but you're hands down the funniest."

A couple of weeks later I was typing and printing away when the printer started going screwy on me. Paper was flying all over the place. I didn't know what to do, so I got out the instruction manual and looked up "Troubleshooting." I turned to the page and there was a lovely pencil sketch of a woman dealing with the printer, telling me to first undo the "papar sepelator." I looked all over for the papar sepelator and couldn't for the life of me locate it. It was late and I didn't want to bother Beth, but I had no choice. Besides, she had given me her home number, saying she was like a doctor—I could call her anytime if there was an emergency.

"Beth, it's Carol. I'm sorry to call you so late, but . . ."

"What's the emergency?"

I explained the situation, and she told me exactly what to do to fix it.

Before we hung up, I asked her what and where the papar sepelator was.

"Have you been looking at the owner's manual?"

"Yes, and I couldn't find the papar sepelator."

She laughed and said that unless I was in love with the artist's sketches, I should toss the book.

"Why? What's wrong with it?"

"It was printed in Japan and translated from Japanese into English. There's no such thing as a papar sepelator in the printer."

I didn't get it.

She repeated it. "Translated from *Japanese* into *English*. Think about it."

I finally got it: PA-PAR SEP-E-LA-TOR = PA-PER SEP-A-RA-TOR.

I thanked her and we hung up. I pressed Mr. Off Button, got into bed, and laughed myself to sleep.

Beverly Sills

*

"Bubbles." It was the perfect nickname for her. I used to say that if there was ever a power outage, I'd want to be with Beverly Sills because her smile could light up the room. And that laugh of hers was like no other, either; it reminded me of bells and wind chimes. Years earlier I had seen Mike Wallace interview Beverly Sills on *60 Minutes*, and I fell in love with that personality of hers on the spot, saying to myself, "I have to meet this amazing woman someday."

Beverly Sills's glorious soprano voice had taken her to the highest pinnacles an opera singer can reach. Her private life was another matter. Though she had a good solid marriage with her husband, Peter Greenough, their son, Bucky, was born severely impaired, and was institutionalized at a very young age. Their beautiful daughter, Muffy, was born deaf. Neither one of Beverly's children ever had the thrill of hearing their mother sing. The irony was not to be believed, but there it was.

During the *60 Minutes* interview, Mike Wallace brought up the subject of her children and asked Beverly how, with all this

*Beverly Sills and me singing the blues
on the Metropolitan Opera stage.*

tragedy, she always seemed to be so happy. She replied that she wasn't necessarily happy, but that she always tried to be cheerful.

Cheerful. That was her mantra.

In 1976 I was planning another special for CBS, so I called Beverly's manager, Edgar Vincent, and asked him to test the waters and see if she would like to get into the sandbox and play with me. We had never met, but I admired her so much I was willing to take the chance. Within minutes, she returned the call herself.

"Carol?"

"Miss Sills?"

"It's Bubbles. When can we play together?"

I was floored. She was saying yes.

She was coming out to LA for a brief visit, so we set up a time when we could meet and talk about the kind of show we'd like to do. Laughing, she said she'd be staying at the "Beverly Sills Hotel."

I drove up the hotel's long driveway and there she was, waiting for me out front. She got in the car and gave me that big smile and a bigger hug. We started talking and giggling at once and didn't stop until we got to my house. It was as if we'd known each other our whole lives.

Ken and Mitzie Welch, who were going to write all the musical special material for the show, were waiting for us, along with Joe, who would produce. Out of that meeting came *Sills and Burnett at the Met*.

It was a joyous time from that very first meeting. We laughed all through rehearsals, opened with a comedy number, "We're Only an Octave Apart," did sketches, and wound up with a tap-dancing finale that brought the house down. As I've said many times before, I'm a nut for bad weather, and whenever I've done a show for the first time it has either snowed or rained. I remember telling the crew, the dancers, and of course Beverly on

March 9, the day before the show, to bundle up the next night when we taped, because "we're gonna have some weather!" I don't think it was predicted, but the next day New York welcomed a MAJOR snowstorm!

The show couldn't have gone better. It wound up winning some wonderful reviews and quite a few awards. We both cried when it was over.

Over the years, whenever I went to New York I would call Bubbles before I had even unpacked. We would get together often. When I was back in California, we called each other constantly. In spite of any personal anguish she was going through, she was always cheerful.

Once again, I got my wish. I not only got to meet Beverly Sills, but over the years we developed a loving friendship that cheers my heart whenever I think of her . . . which is every single day.

She died in 2007.

How blessed I am to have known her.

And if there *is* something after this life, I can't wait to get back into the sandbox with her and play some more. One thing I do know: it's sure to snow.

Questions and Answers
on the Road

*

As I mentioned in the introduction, for quite a few years now I've been taking to the road with the same Q & A format that I used to open our variety show every week. I never know what the questions will be, so it forces me to be in the moment. My mind can't wander for a second. Many of the questions are about our show and Tim, Harvey, Vicki, and Lyle, which I welcome because I have several stories I can tell.

And then there are those questions that just throw me for a loop.

* * *

A while back I was in Pennsylvania and a young man raised his hand.

"Yes, the young man on the aisle."

"It's my twenty-fifth birthday today. Would you give me a birthday hug?"

"Sure. Come on up."

The young man bounded up onto the stage, whereupon I gave him a big hug and asked the audience to sing "Happy Birthday." He thanked me and returned to his seat. It was a nice moment, and a few minutes later I called on a handsome gentleman dressed in a nice suit and tie. He stood up and said, "Miss Burnett, I'm not twenty-five but it's my birthday, too, and I'd like a hug because I've always found you to be a most attractive lady."

I knew I could have some fun with him, so I shouted, "No kidding? What're you waiting for? Get up here!" The audience was laughing as he made his way onstage. He came for me with his arms outstretched for THE HUG. I held him back with my hands and said, "Now wait a minute, not so fast! We hardly know each other!" He backed off, a little red in the face.

The audience was having as much fun as I was. I continued, "So how old are you today?"

"Forty."

"Forty. And what's your name?"

"Bob."

"Thank you for the nice compliment, Bob. And you want a hug?"

He started for me again and I held him off again, much to the audience's delight. "Sooo, tell me, Bob, have you ever thought in terms of an older woman?"

He took a couple of steps back, and the audience howled.

"What's the matter, Bob?"

"N-Nothing."

"Oh no! Bob, are you trying to tell me you're involved with someone else?"

"Sort of . . ." The audience was eating this up.

"Sort of? I don't understand, Bob. What do you mean, 'sort of'?"

There was a short pause.

"I'm a priest."

* * *

Another time I was in Texas and a woman in the balcony asked me the weirdest question ever. She must have been working on it for a long time.

"Carol, if you could be a member of the opposite sex for twenty-four hours, and then pop back and be yourself again, who would you be and what would you do?"

My mind started racing like mad. Opposite sex? For twenty-four hours? Who would I be? What would I do? I said a quick little prayer. *Please, let me just open my mouth and have whatever comes out make sense.*

I took a deep breath and what came out was this:

"I'd be Osama bin Laden, and I'd kill myself."

Brian

*

In 1993 I signed on to perform for six weeks in a musical in
Long Beach, and met Brian Miller. He was the contractor
who hired the musicians and also played drums for this particular production. Musicians have always been special to me, not
only for their unique talents but also for their sense of humor.
During rehearsals the cast and crew would take a break and relax downstairs around the coffee machine. I was drawn to Brian
because he was fun, smart, and easy to be around. I began to
look forward to those coffee breaks.

After the show closed we went our separate ways.

A few years later we ran into each other at an outdoor mall
in Los Angeles. Lunch followed, and then a movie, and then dinner. Despite our age difference (he's quite a bit younger than I
am), I thought of Brian as a contemporary. He knew and loved
all the old movies I had grown up with, and was even able to
quote from them at length. And as far as music goes . . . well, he
knew just about every standard written. All of that, along with
being a classically trained musician and the drummer for the

Brian and me.
COURTESY OF CAROL BURNETT

Hollywood Bowl Orchestra for several years, made him very appealing.

After a few months I introduced Brian to my girls, and they took to him instantly, which made me very happy. Next it was time for him to meet the gang—Harvey, Tim, and their wives. We all gathered for dinner at an Italian restaurant in Beverly Hills.

Harvey, slipping into the role of my father, said later that he had been reluctant to meet my new beau for fear that he might be all wrong for me. Happily, it turned out to be a terrific evening, and we all wound up laughing and hugging on the sidewalk while we were waiting for our cars. And the best part of all was Harvey planting a big kiss on Brian's cheek, saying, "Welcome to the family."

Brian and I tied the knot in November 2001.

It rained that day.

In addition to his work as a drummer, Brian is one of Los Angeles's busiest contractors of musicians for theater and live events, and he also acts as personnel manager for one of the city's resident orchestras, all of which keeps him pretty busy. He's brilliantly funny and makes me laugh constantly. What's most important is that I feel safe with him. He's a loving human being, and my very best friend.

A side note: we're both a lot like Felix Unger (the neatnik in *The Odd Couple*). There are even times when we come close to arm-wrestling over the Windex bottle!

Pets

✳

A few years ago I was working in a Broadway play, *Moon over Buffalo*. It got a little lonely in my hotel room between shows, so I began to think about getting a dog to keep me company. I mentioned it to a few of our cast members and crew, and they made me see the light. First of all, I would have to "hotel-break" a puppy. Then I'd have to get up every morning at the crack of dawn to walk him/her (it was winter), repeat the procedure in the afternoon, and then do it once again when I got back late at night after the curtain. It would be almost like taking care of a baby.

The solution was obvious: a cat. They only require food, water, a litter box, and of course TLC. How would I know what kind to get? The answer was simple: "The cat chooses *you*."

So the following Monday (our day off), I found myself at an animal shelter on the East Side, Bide-a-Wee. It had been recommended to me because they never put their animals to sleep. They kept them alive and cared for them even if they were never chosen. I could see that some of the animals were up there in years, and I thought, "What a wonderful group of people. I've come to the right place."

I told the manager that I was there to adopt a cat. She took me down to where the felines were housed, a long hallway lined with cages on both sides, full of kitties of all kinds. I walked down the hall checking out the cages on my right, and then up the hall checking them out on my left. They were all so adorable that I swear I wanted to work there! I spotted two beautiful Siamese kittens sleeping wrapped around each other. I asked about them and the manager said they'd come in together and the shelter wouldn't split them up. I appreciated Bide-a-Wee even more.

I asked her, "How do I choose one? They're all wonderful." Same reply. "The cat chooses *you!*"

So up and down the hall I went once again.

I was peeking at a sleeping kitten on the right when I heard a meow behind me and turned around to see a beautiful pair of eyes staring at me. I approached this cat's cage to peer in, and her front paw reached through the bars and touched my arm. "Hell-ooo! Here I am! Let's go home!"

And that's how I met Roxy. I named her after a character in *Moon over Buffalo.* She was part Maine coon and part something else, I'm not sure what. She was black and white and fluffy, and about four months old.

She was *it.*

So Roxy and I settled into the hotel with all the necessary equipment and food. She slept with me the first night, cuddling up against my neck. We had already bonded. I decided to take her to the theater every night so she wouldn't be alone. I bought a second litter box and put it in our little dressing room, just in case. She immediately became a kind of mascot. My dresser for the show, Laura Beattie, was a cat person, and it wasn't long before Roxy was as comfortable in our dressing room as she was at the hotel.

Unfortunately, she got a little *too* comfortable.

Roxy and me.
COURTESY OF CAROL BURNETT

As time went on, for some reason the finale music that played during the curtain calls triggered Roxy to leave a few "calling cards" in the litter box, thereby stinking up the entire dressing room, whose one window had been painted shut for years. This happened every night for the rest of the run. Was it the time of day or the sound of the music that stirred her up? The show itself?

No matter—until we closed, I made it a point to greet guests coming backstage outside in the hall.

I didn't want them to think it was me.

Roxy died a short while later. Something had been wrong with her since she was born, so she only lived for three years. It broke my heart.

I have her ashes in a little container on a shelf in my den.

* * *

It took me a while, but I began to think about getting another cat—not to replace Roxy, but to give another little critter my love. I had heard about how smart and loving the Bengal breed is, so I checked it out on the computer. (Yep, Beth, I can surf the Web now!) Brian and I visited a breeder and met their Bengal family, consisting of Mama, Papa, and their brood of four. The first three kittens seemed to be in audition mode—jumping, doing flips, rolling over, and all but tap-dancing to be noticed. The fourth was rather quiet and proceeded to climb onto my lap and curl up for a nap. I handed her to Brian and she snuggled into his neck. Yes, she had picked us. "Hell-ooo! Here I am! Let's go home!"

Here's Mabel, kicking back.
COURTESY OF CAROL BURNETT

So along came Mabel. I named her after Nanny. She's a beautiful cat with jade-green eyes, tiger-like stripes, and a personality that makes me howl with laughter.

That was ten years ago. Mabel talks, fetches (!), and curls up on my lap when I'm reading the paper or watching television. She follows Brian and me around the house, and will come to us when we call her. My favorite Mabel quirk occurs when it's time to eat: if she hasn't been fed yet, she lifts the receiver off the telephone. "Hello, room service?"

I look at it this way: Roxy gave me everything she could in her short lifetime. And she opened my heart to the possibility that became Mabel.

God bless our furry loved ones.

Hal Prince,
Hollywood Arms,
Carrie

*

"The Prince of Broadway" was the clue in the *New York Times* crossword puzzle. The answer? Director-producer Hal Prince. *A prince of a talent, and a prince of a man.*

As I've mentioned, back in 1986 Random House published my first book, *One More Time.* It wasn't about show business. It was about growing up in an eccentric, alcoholic, dysfunctional, yet loving household. It was a personal journal to share with my kids. The book came out and sold well, and I retired it to my bookshelf.

In 1998 my daughter Carrie called me from her home in Colorado. At thirty-five she had a good career going: guest-starring in movies for television, writing, and singing. She had an idea she wanted to pitch to me.

"Mom, I think we could take the first part of *One More Time* and make a play out of it. Just for the fun of it. You and me, together. How about it?"

Just for the fun of it.

Hal and me at Chicago rehearsals for Hollywood Arms.
COURTESY OF CAROL BURNETT

We began collaborating long-distance. Carrie would write in her Colorado mountain cabin and I would write in my Los Angeles apartment. The faxes flew back and forth. Nanny, Mama, and Daddy were all coming to life. Carrie was getting to know her family in the most profound way, putting dialogue to moments that echoed in my deepest memories. She had never known these people in life, but she knew them now—not by writing about them, but by writing *them*.

After some theater lab workshops with the Sundance Theater

and the help of workshop director Philip Himberg, we were ready to show the play to some producers and directors. We got some interest from a producer who suggested two highly respected Broadway directors. Carrie and I didn't have a clue about which one to pursue, so I called my friend Hal Prince for advice. He knew and admired both directors, so he asked if he could read the play before giving us a recommendation.

He read it and offered to direct it himself! Hal Prince. The director of *Phantom of the Opera, Evita, Cabaret, Sweeney Todd, Follies, Company,* and countless other Broadway successes, the winner of over twenty Tony Awards, wanted to work with *us* on our little play.

Carrie and I were over the moon.

Over the next couple of years, Hal helped us turn our work into a real stage play. Originally we had written lots of scenes in many different settings—the one-room apartment Nanny and I had lived in, Mama's room down the hall, the rooftop of the apartment building, Daddy's hospital room, and so on. It was more like a movie than a stage play. Our first assignment from Hal was to put all the action in our one-room apartment and on the rooftop. Hal said, "Confinement is your friend." Was he ever right.

Carrie was still in Colorado, I was in LA, and now Hal was in New York. Once again, the faxes flew. We found out that the apartment building Nanny and I had lived in when we moved out from San Antonio had been called Hollywood Arms when it was first built in the twenties. We had our title.

Hal sent the play to Robert Falls, the artistic director of the Goodman Theatre in Chicago, and we were offered a limited run beginning in April 2002.

Then Carrie got sick.

Carrie was diagnosed with lung cancer in the summer of 2001. Determined to beat it, she moved back to Los Angeles, where she insisted on driving herself to her chemotherapy and radiation treatments. During these first few months we continued working with Hal on *Hollywood Arms*. Carrie was in and out of the hospital, rallying and getting sprung to go home.

I remember one of the times Carrie was readmitted to Cedars-Sinai, in the late fall of 2001. I entered her hospital room. It was around five in the morning and she was stirring. I looked down at her as she opened her eyes and smiled at me. Looking around the room, I feebly joked, "So you wanted to come back here again, huh?"

"I missed the food."

For a while there, we all believed she'd lick it—Carrie most of all.

One of the nurses asked her how come she smiled so much.

She replied, "Every day I wake up and decide: today I'm going to love my life."

COURTESY OF CAROL BURNETT

Obituary

*

January 21, 2002

CARRIE HAMILTON *(December 1963–January 2002)*

Carrie Hamilton, an actress, writer and musician and a daughter of Carol Burnett, died yesterday. She was 38.

The cause was cancer.

Ms. Hamilton, whose father was the late producer Joe Hamilton, appeared in the television series "Fame" and had guest roles on other shows, including "Murder She Wrote," "Beverly Hills 90210" and "thirtysomething." She also starred in television movies.

She and her mother collaborated on a stage version of Ms. Burnett's best-selling memoir "One More Time." The resulting play, "Hollywood Arms," is scheduled to have its world premiere in Chicago in April.

Ms. Hamilton spoke publicly in the 1980's about her struggles with addiction and her decision to go drug free.

She starred as Maureen in the first national touring

version of the musical "Rent," had feature film credits and wrote and directed short films through the profit-sharing production company Namethkuf. She won "The Women in Film Award" at the 2001 Latino Film Festival for her short film "Lunchtime Thomas."

Ms. Hamilton is survived by two sisters, Erin and Jody Hamilton, and by Ms. Burnett. *(New York Times)*

I didn't want to get out of bed.

I had the support of my family and friends and my dear husband, Brian, yet having the covers over my face gave me whatever small comfort I could find.

Hal called. The play was set to open in Chicago at the Goodman Theatre in late April, and it wasn't yet finished. It was time to get back to work.

Still I stayed in bed, until Brian told me in no uncertain terms that I owed it to Carrie, I owed it to myself, and I owed it to Hal, who had nurtured and carried *Hollywood Arms*, Carrie, and me all this way.

"It's time to throw off the covers, Carol," he said.

Flying to Chicago to begin rehearsals, I held on to Brian's hand, closed my eyes, and prayed. *Carrie, let me know you're with me. Give me a sign. I need you to help me through these next few weeks. I need your strength.* Brian and I checked into the hotel room, where a huge bouquet was waiting for me: "Welcome to Chicago. See you tomorrow. Love, Hal." It was a beautiful array of birds-of-paradise. I nearly fell over. Hal had no idea that was Carrie's favorite flower—she even had one tattooed on her shoulder. This was definitely a sign.

The next night, after the first rehearsal, Hal, Brian, and I went out to dinner at a lovely restaurant downtown. The maître d' offered us a special brand of champagne as a welcome-to-Chicago gift. He showed us the label. There was a name on it: Louise. *My mother's name and Carrie's middle name!* I had what I needed to keep me going.

Hollywood Arms went on to open on Broadway October 31, 2002, starring Linda Lavin (brilliant as Nanny), Michele Pawk (heartbreaking as Mama), and Frank Wood (so very touching as Daddy). It closed early in 2003, winning a Tony Award for the beautiful Michele. My baby and I had gone the distance, thanks to Hal.

I quote John Simon's final paragraph in his review of *Hollywood Arms.*

> But *Hollywood Arms* has yet another form of invaluable affection, that of Harold Prince for the characters and their story. You will never see more feelingful insight, more self-effacing love for their quirks, foibles, and kindnesses from a director for his stage children, big and small. If only this thoroughly endearing play and production could have been seen by Miss Burnett's daughter and co-author, Carrie Hamilton, dead before even the Goodman Theatre premiere. One fervently hopes that the joy of such a true creation accompanied her on her final journey.

Not surprisingly, perhaps, it was Carrie who best described what she left behind.

> *Our legacy is really the lives we touch, the inspiration we give, altering someone's plan—if even for a moment—and getting them to think, cry, laugh, argue. More than anything, we are remembered for our smiles; the ones we share with our closest and dearest, and the ones we bestow on a total stranger, who needed it RIGHT THEN, and God put you there to deliver.*

Carrie and the Fib

*

There are times when I'm thinking about Carrie and a particularly funny story comes to mind, taking me back to when she was a little girl.

We had caught Carrie in a fib. I don't even remember what it was exactly, but Joe and I felt it was important to send her upstairs to her room right after dinner. It couldn't have been much of a lie. She was only five, but we wanted to make sure it registered with her that fibbing was not a good thing.

After a few minutes I knocked on the door and entered the bedroom she shared with Jody. We were alone. She was in her PJs and under the covers. She had been crying. I sat on the edge of the bed and bent over and kissed her, wiping the tears away.

"Sweetheart, your daddy and I love you very much. You know that, don't you?"

"Uh-huh . . ."

"We love you, but we don't like what you *did*. Do you understand the difference?"

She nodded. I moved closer. "Honey, you can *always* tell us the truth, no matter what, and we'll still love you. That will *never* change. "

She was staring at me. Hard. I moved even closer. Face-to-face.

"It's just that telling fibs or lies can only lead to bigger fibs and bigger lies and then things get worse and worse—and we don't want that, now, do we?"

Carrie hadn't blinked or taken her eyes off me. I was really getting through to her. By this time we were nose to nose. I seized the opportunity to expand on the importance of honest communication, moving on to talk about how love could over-come any differences we might have. "Never be afraid to come and talk to us about anything. I promise Daddy and I will listen, and we will work it out, no matter what it is."

She was looking at me, mesmerized. This had been going on for several minutes and she was still drinking in what I was saying, with all her heart! I was so proud of myself and of how I was handling the situation that, I swear, in the back of my mind I heard *violins*. Somebody, somewhere, was about to present me with a medal for Mother of the Year.

I finally finished, and asked Carrie if she had anything to ask me.

"Uh-huh."

"What, darling? Anything. Just ask."

"How many teeth do you have?"

What's Next?

✳

I've had a great run. I've had the highest of highs and the
lowest of lows, both professionally and personally. When I
need inspiration, I think of Beverly Sills and do my best to
emulate her, to concentrate on all the wonderful times I've had
and continue to have, living my dreams to the fullest.

My dear friend Mitzie Welch told me that when she's going
to sleep every night, she counts at least three Gratefuls for the
day she has just lived through. It's a pretty good idea.

I'm happily married to Brian, for which I count a Grateful
every day.

I lost my beautiful Carrie, yet I was blessed to have had her
light in my life. I feel her presence daily, and for that I count a
Grateful, too.

My Jody and Erin are loving and beautiful inside and out;
two more Gratefuls.

Erin is the mom of my grandsons, two smart and healthy
boys, Zach and Dylan. Grateful and Grateful.

My sister, Chrissy, and I are still very close. Grateful.

Jody, grandson Zach, Erin, and grandson Dylan.
COURTESY OF CAROL BURNETT

I'm alive and healthy. Grateful.

I still work doing the occasional guest shot on TV, a movie here and there, and the Q & A's on the road—nothing taxing, and it suits me fine (even more Gratefuls).

As for the career, sometimes I catch myself daydreaming about being young again and doing it all over. Then I bring myself up short when I realize how incredibly fortunate I was. What we had in the 1960s and 1970s couldn't be duplicated on television today. Joe was a wonderful producer, and CBS put a tremendous amount of faith in us. These days, in my opinion, there's too much network interference, and shows that don't make it in the first couple of weeks are often cancelled before they have a chance to find an audience.

Starting out today, would I really have been able to do all the musical TV specials with the amazing friends and talents with whom I had the thrill of working? Would a network support the idea of guest stars, dancers and singers, comedy sketches, elaborate sets, fifty costumes a week, and a full LIVE twenty-eight-piece orchestra? With real violins and drums and no synthesizers?

The answer is no. No way could I find these opportunities today. Nothing like our show (and, I might add, all the other variety shows during that time) could ever see the light of day today. The networks just aren't there for that kind of programming anymore. They won't spend the money—and, given the profusion of cable competitors, they may not even have the money. And, sad to say, audiences won't even know what they're missing unless they look for the old variety show reruns late at night on some distant cable channel.

So I add to my Gratefuls that my time happened when it did.

And I'm grateful I can look back and say once more, "I'm so glad we had this time together."

Acknowledgments

My thanks to Shaye Areheart, a publisher whose encouragement and smarts made this experience a joy.

I would also like to thank my editor, Peter Guzzardi, for his guidance and TLC along the way.

About the Type

The text of this book was set in Bell, a Transitional typeface created for Monotype in 1931 and originally cut by Richard Austin in 1788 for John Bell's type foundry. When Bell's foundry closed down, the font migrated for decades under different names: "English Copperplate" at the American Riverside Press in 1792, then "Brimmer," and later "Mountjoye," until font designer Stanley Morrison restored the name again in 1931. Unique to Bell is its break from tradition for numerals: They are two thirds the height of the font's capitals and sit evenly on the line.